Aberdeenshire

40 Coast & Country Walks

The authors and publisher have made every effort to ensure that the information in this publication is accurate, and accept no responsibility whatsoever for any loss, injury or inconvenience experienced by any person or persons whilst using this book.

published by
pocket mountains ltd
The Old Church, Annanside,
Moffat, Dumfries and Galloway DG10 9EB
pocketmountains.com

ISBN: 978-1-916739-05-5

Text and photography copyright © Helen and Paul Webster

First published 2011. This revised edition published 2025

Printed by J Thomson Colour Printers, Glasgow

Introduction

This guide covers Scotland's third largest city, Aberdeen, and the surrounding rolling countryside and dramatic coastline. Stretching from the massive dunes of Collieston in the north to the wide arc of sand at St Cyrus in the south, this volume takes a big bite out of rural Aberdeenshire – featuring the popular moorland peaks of Bennachie, the Deeside settlements of Banchory and Aboyne and north to Huntly, Turriff and Fyvie where castles dot the agricultural landscape. The area known as Royal Deeside, which includes Ballater and Braemar, forms part of the Cairngorms National Park – walks in this area can be found in the companion guidebook, **Aviemore and the Cairngorms: 40 Shorter Walks**; likewise, walks around the picturesque fishing villages of North Aberdeenshire can be found in the guide, **Moray: 40 Coast and Country Walks**.

Most of the walks in this guide are straightforward and can be completed in a morning or afternoon. The landscape and contrast between city and countryside means variety is the key to this selection of both much loved and less known outings. Aberdeen itself offers a rich history and architecture-laden tours exploring different areas of the city, including its golden beach. The rural routes are mainly circuits and, where possible, include access by public transport. In addition to the coast, Aberdeenshire has more than its fair share of characterful small hills, most with stunning views: some of these routes do necessitate an up and back approach, in which case the time given is the estimated time for the whole route without stops.

Many walks are designed to be combined with visits to local attractions, castles, distilleries and the numerous tearooms, cafés and pubs in these areas. A good number of the routes are perfect for adventurous families, with highlights including the chance to play king of the castle at Dunnottar, endless open space and a small petting zoo at Hazlehead Park in Aberdeen, a tower to climb atop Scolty Hill and the chance for little legs to run on the great expanses of sand at St Cyrus.

A sketch map accompanies each route, many of which are waymarked, well-walked and established routes with little chance of getting lost as long as you are properly prepared; however, an Ordnance Survey map is usually advised. Where the routes are likely to be muddy underfoot, this is highlighted, but in general decent waterproof footwear should be worn on most of the walks. Waterproofs and extra clothing are essential on some of the hillier walks, such as Bennachie or Clachnaben, where weather conditions can change very rapidly.

General access information and dogs

Scotland has some of the most walker-friendly rights in the world with access permitted over most land away from residential buildings. With these rights come responsibilities, as set out in the

Scottish Outdoor Access Code, essentially requiring respect for other land users and responsible access, especially on farmed or grazing land. In particular, dogs should be kept on short leads or under tight control during the spring and early summer to stop them disturbing livestock and ground-nesting birds. Dogs should also be kept away from livestock at all times.

The people and the land

Fit like? Doric, which is used nowadays to refer to the mid-northern Scots dialect, is still in use today, particularly in North Aberdeenshire, Fraserburgh and Peterhead with variations in other parts. So if someone asks 'Ay ay, fit like?' or 'Fou's yer doos?', it means 'how are you?' (the latter literally means 'how are your pigeons?').

The surviving dialect is one pointer to the region's long history, as Aberdeen and its shire has seen human habitation since prehistoric times. The area is dotted with ancient sites, cairns, cists, forts, standing stones and stone circles, all testament to its early inhabitants.

Aberdeen itself is an ancient city, built up around a small fishing port on the Dee Estuary and the area now known as Old Aberdeen around the mouth of the Don. Fishing has remained important in the northern settlements of Fraserburgh and Peterhead, but is much diminished in Aberdeen itself. A stroll around Footdee reveals the picturesque former fishertown close to the sea where the houses, designed with net drying, fish gutting

and net mending in mind, huddle together in a tight-knit hollow just metres from the North Sea.

Much of Aberdeen's early prosperity came from shipbuilding and sea-going trade, as well as a thriving textile and paper industry. These traditional industries were eclipsed by the boom years following the discovery of North Sea oil. This in turn has sparked the growth of high-end property and shopping, both evident on any tour of the city centre or outlying suburbs and villages. Many of the buildings in the centre date from the Victorian era, built using the locally quarried granite that gives Aberdeen its nickname, 'the Granite City'. Granite is a famously hard rock and as a result many of the buildings still look almost as new; however, the grey rock can give the city an austere face, despite the sparkling of the mica in the rock in the rain. Aberdeen is also one of the few cities to boast a wide sandy beach, although the east coast weather, despite being often sunny, is rarely without a bracing breeze – the sands are usually more popular with surfers, joggers and dog walkers than those seeking a Bermudian tan.

The city is blessed with fine parks and open spaces, and two walks include visits to Duthie Park, where the wonderful (and tropically warm) Winter Gardens should not be missed, and Hazlehead Park where there is a plethora of activities on offer, including golf courses, a huge children's play area, maze and pet's corner.

Inland from the city, the richness of the

agricultural land becomes apparent in the patchwork of fields, watered by the Rivers Dee and Don, with the occasional moorland hill poking up above as the great massif of the Cairngorms is approached. Some 4000 years ago, man first began to grow crops and domesticate livestock in this area. Many of the relics from the prehistoric eras remain archaeological mysteries, and good examples such as the recumbent Tomnaverie Stone Circle near Tarland can be seen on these walks. Later examples of Bronze Age fortified hillforts dating back to 2200BC can be seen on Mither Tap and Dunnideer near Insch.

Natural history

Having such a varied landscape, Aberdeenshire abounds with different natural habitats. The wild cliffs, as well as providing excellent sites for towering man-made castles and fortresses, offer nesting sites for thousands of seabirds. The Bullers of Buchan are particularly spectacular during late spring and early summer when the air turns white with wheeling birds. However, the other coastal routes are also good for wildlife spotting, with the Ythan Estuary known for its wading birds and the dunes at Balmedie another rich habitat. The coast is also a great spot for looking out for seals, porpoise or dolphins, with Boddam Head a favourite location.

Inland, Aberdeenshire remains a stronghold of the red squirrel, and efforts to eradicate its grey sibling, which carries a virus that threatens much of the population of reds in the North East, have seen considerable success. Look out for the red-tufted creatures on any of the woodland walks. Another seasonal spectacular is the salmon leaping as they make their way upriver to traditional spawning grounds; the Falls of Feugh, near the start of the Scolty Hill walk, is a good place to watch for this during October and November each year.

Fly fishing for these wily creatures, as well as brown trout, remains very popular on the wide rivers of the area, particularly the Dee. Combined with golf and shooting, and the many excellent teashops, castles and whisky distilleries nearby, the area has a very traditional feel. However, the vibrant pulse from the university and technology-driven city of Aberdeen and the changing use of the countryside, including the increasing popularity of sports such as mountain biking and kite surfing, means there is something for everyone.

Oldmeldrum

Newburgh

Inverurie

A947

A90

A96

8

7

A944

3

Aberdeen

5

1

A93

2

4

6

A90

Peterculter

Stonehaven

Walking offers the opportunity to explore the bustling Granite City at a slower pace, with time to look up at the imposing buildings, gaze out to sea or muse on times long gone. To residents and visitors alike, an exploration on foot will always reveal unexpected sights and sounds.

The rich heritage of Aberdeen is celebrated in each of the city walks. The real buzz of the city can be felt on a walk around its city centre, a metropolitan mix of cafés, bars, galleries, museums and more shops than you could ever need. Take your eye off the latest bargains and designer offerings to discover a surprising array of sculptures and fine granite architecture. The longest route takes in the immense sandy beach before delving into the cobbled streets of Old Aberdeen, home to the grand buildings of Scotland's third university. In the tiny, cramped wynds of the old fishing village of Footdee, it is easy to imagine the fisherfolk that once would have gathered to mend and dry nets, gut fish, hang out washing and gossip. The short walk from the city centre passes the hulks of the modern ships which help make Aberdeen one of the busiest ports in the UK. The shipping traffic can be watched from the walk around the headland of Girdle Ness, a bracing escape from the centre with its lighthouse still protecting lives as it shines its beam out across the North Sea.

If your route-finding skills are up to it, head to Hazlehead Park to immerse yourself in Scotland's oldest maze. A perfect outing for families, Hazlehead offers a walk through both woodland and more formal gardens. Duthie Park is famed for its Winter Gardens and is the starting point for a much rougher walk alongside the Dee, whilst just beyond the city limits there are a variety of forestry walks with brisk climbs and great views.

Union Terrace Gardens ▶

Aberdeen

Granite City

Distance 3.25km **Time** 1 hour
Terrain city streets with pavement
Map OS Explorer 406 **Access** Aberdeen is
well served by buses and trains

**Saunter around the best of Aberdeen's
granite buildings and civic sculptures,
allowing extra time if you want to visit
the city's excellent art gallery and Provost
Skene's House along the way.**

Aberdeen is built on granite and much of
its early wealth came from exporting this
hard rock. The durable stone stands up to
the test of time and, in the sunshine after a
rain shower, the granite city really does
sparkle. This meander around the city
centre starts at the Mercat Cross in
Castlegate at the east end of Castle/ Union
Street. Dating from 1686, the hexagonal
structure topped by a unicorn was where
everyone gathered for markets, public
punishments and royal proclamations.

From here, pass the Gordon Highlanders
statue and cross the road to the columned
entrance of The Archibald Simpson, now a
pub named after the architect of this
former bank building. He also built
Aberdeen's St Andrew's Cathedral, part of
Marischal College and many other local
landmarks. Continue along Castle Street,
passing opposite the Castlegate Well, on
which sits a lead figure known locally as
The Mannie, before turning right into
Broad Street. After a crossing, you reach
Marischal College – the second largest
granite building in the world. It blends the
more austere style of Archibald Simpson
from the 1830s with the 'perpendicular
gothic' style (1904-06) of Alexander
Marshall Mackenzie. Built for the
University of Aberdeen, it now houses
Aberdeen City Council offices. Cross the
road at Marischal Square and head for
Provost Skene's House in an attractive
courtyard. The house is well worth a visit –
parts date back to 1545, and it includes the
remarkable Painted Gallery, its ceilings
covered with a cycle of religious paintings.

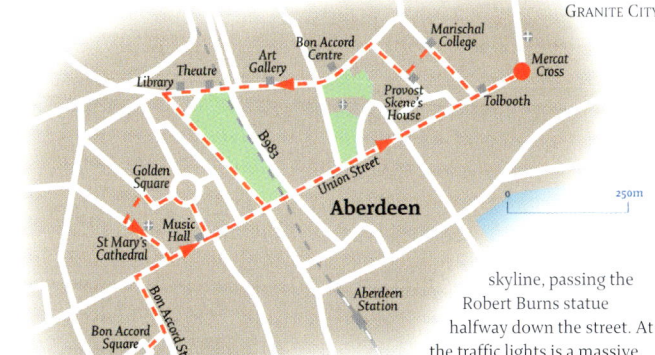

Aberdeen

250m

◄ Mercat Cross

Make sure you sneak a look up at the Russell Head on the building's corner behind the statue of football legend Denis Law. George Russell, an aggrieved landlord whose tenant's bakery was closed down by the council in the 1860s, had this effigy of himself carved and fixed at the bakery to glower endlessly at a neighbour he believed to be responsible for its closure; the head was moved here in 1959. Pass the bronze sculpture of two dancing figures and turn right into Flourmill Lane. At Upper Kirkgate, bear left down onto Schoolhill, passing Robert Gordon's College and then the city art gallery. On the far corner of the art gallery is the war memorial with its majestic granite lion.

Continue ahead towards His Majesty's Theatre and the central library, seen on the opposite side of the road. Just before the library is an impressive statue of William Wallace. Cut left here up the steps to Prince Albert on his throne, and now follow imposing Union Terrace with its views over the gardens to the Aberdeen skyline, passing the Robert Burns statue halfway down the street. At the traffic lights is a massive statue of King Edward VII looking suitably regal on a red Peterhead granite plinth. Turn right onto Union Street and take the second on the right, South Silver Street, to reach Golden Square, where a statue of the 5th and last Duke of Gordon stands in the centre of an elegant square of granite townhouses. Head left to leave via Crimon Place and, after this bends right, aim slightly left to follow a path around the back and side of St Mary's Cathedral, emerging onto Huntly Street.

A left turn past the front of the cathedral quickly brings you back to Union Street. Turn right and, after making your way over the busy road at the crossing, turn left down Bon Accord Street. The second on the right reaches Bon Accord Square, composed of Georgian homes built by Archibald Simpson for some of the city's wealthier residents in the 1820s with a memorial stone (granite, of course) to Simpson himself in the centre. Return to Union Street and this time turn right, passing the columns of the Music Hall on the far side and continuing all the way back to the Mercat Cross at the far end.

Footdee and Aberdeen Harbour

Distance 4.75km **Time** 1 hour 30
Terrain streets with pavements
Map OS Explorer 406 **Access** Aberdeen is
well served by buses and trains

**Explore the cottages of the former fishing
village of Footdee, locally pronounced
'Fittie', to get a feel for this important part
of Aberdeen's heritage. The walk from
the city centre passes the massive ships
of the modern-day harbour and also takes
in the sandy beach.**

This route starts at the top of Shiprow,
off Union Street, a short walk west of
Aberdeen's Mercat Cross in the heart of the
city centre. Head down Shiprow, following
the sign for the Maritime Museum and
harbour. Keep straight on as it joins a
cobbled road and, opposite the Maritime
Museum, go left onto Shore Brae to reach
busy Virginia Street. Bear left to the

pedestrian crossing and on the far side
take Regent Quay, passing a selection of
fine old merchant buildings on the left and
the bustling industrial harbour to the right.

Aberdeen Harbour is one of the busiest
in the UK, handling four million tonnes of
cargo annually, as well as being the port for
the regular ferries to Orkney and Shetland
and the boats that service the offshore oil
industry. The road becomes Waterloo
Quay; continue to a left turn onto York
Place. Soon after, turn right at a crossroads
with York Street and, at the end of an
industrial area, head left at a T-junction,
then right down New Pier Road.

The building with the clockface on the
quay is known as the Roundhouse and was
a navigation control centre dating back to
the end of the 18th century. It has since
been replaced by the striking Marine
Operations Centre a short distance beyond.

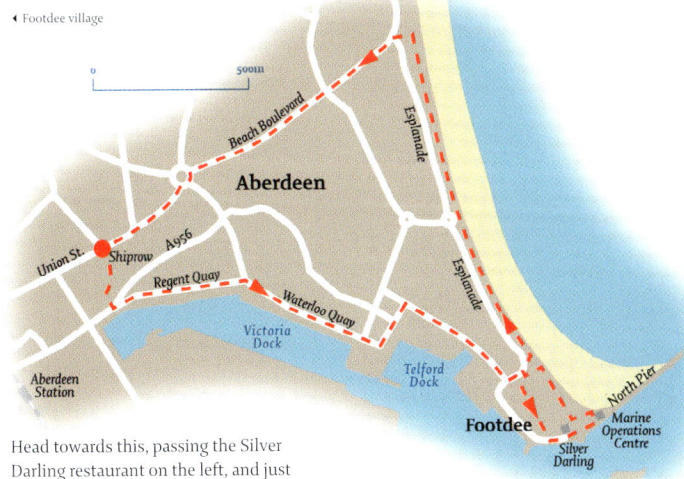

◀ Footdee village

Aberdeen

Beach Boulevard

Esplanade

Esplanade

Union St.

Shiprow

A956

Regent Quay

Waterloo Quay

Victoria Dock

Telford Dock

Aberdeen Station

Footdee

Silver Darling

North Pier

Marine Operations Centre

0   500m

Head towards this, passing the Silver Darling restaurant on the left, and just before reaching the new building turn left to cross a small park. Another left turn immediately after the playpark brings you back to the left of the first stone houses of Footdee. Turn right through the gap to explore the first narrow street.

There has been a fishing village on this site since medieval times, although the present buildings date back to the early 19th century. Once only fisherfolk would have lived here and the small inward-facing houses would have been alive with the sounds and smells of fish drying, processing and net mending. The dense cluster of houses, sheds and immaculate gardens can be explored at your leisure. Eventually, leave Footdee at the far north end and turn left to return to the top of New Pier Road, but this time turn right uphill, passing the public toilets.

Now follow the esplanade behind Aberdeen's sandy beach. Though it has a decent sunshine record, it is often served up with a bracing wind. Just after the Codona's amusement park, turn inland and follow the pavement along the left side of Beach Boulevard. At a large roundabout, keep left and use the pedestrian crossing over Commerce Street, taking the next exit off the roundabout onto Justice Street. This leads back to the city centre, emerging at Castlegate with its paved square and Mercat Cross at the east end of Union Street. Here, the Tolbooth strikes an impressive pose amongst the austere granite façades.

Old Aberdeen and the beach

Distance 8km **Time** 2 hours 30
Terrain seafront, roads with pavements,
woodland and riverside paths
Map OS Explorer 406 **Access** Aberdeen is
well served by buses and trains

**Contrast two Aberdonian gems – the
cobbled streets, ancient buildings and
grand university of Old Aberdeen with the
breezy, sandy and often sunny seafront –
plus explore the woodland and riverside
around the ancient Brig o'Balgownie.**

This is a circuit, so it is possible to start
at any point, with buses to the university
in Old Aberdeen as well as to Aberdeen
beach. This description begins from the
seafront where there is on-street parking.
If not using the bus, you could also reach
this point with a brisk 10-minute walk
from the Mercat Cross at the east end of
Union Street, following Beach Boulevard
from the roundabout.

Begin by the art-deco Beach Ballroom
and walk north away from the city along
the promenade. Continue for some
distance to the north end of the sandy
beach. Instead of taking the faint path
ahead, climb up to the left to join the road,
following it to the right. It curves inland
close by the River Don. The estuary is
popular with wading birds – a bird hide can
be visited overlooking the water on the
right. When you reach the main road
junction, turn right and cross the bridge
and then the road. On the opposite side,
take the footpath down to the riverbank,
signed for the Brig o'Balgownie.

After a while, the riverbank path reaches
stone steps. At the top, turn left to cross
the ancient Brig o'Balgownie. In the 13th
century, this granite and sandstone bridge
served as an important trade link on the
military route along the east coast. Pass a
picturesque cluster of cottages and go
through a gate on the right into Seaton
Park Wood. The main path bears right,

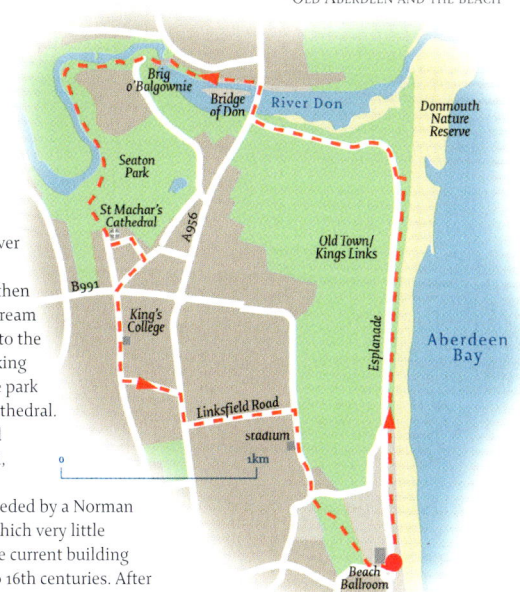

◀ Aberdeen beach

keeping above the River Don as it squeezes through a gorge and then follows the river upstream to Seaton Park. Keep to the main path before forking left to climb up to the park exit at St Machar's Cathedral.

Cross the graveyard to reach the cathedral, founded in 580AD by St Machar and superseded by a Norman cathedral in 1131, of which very little remains – much of the current building dates from the 13th to 16th centuries. After his execution and dismembering in 1305, parts of William Wallace are said to have ended up here and been later buried in the walls, though the present church had not been built by then.

Leave by the main exit onto The Chanonry, turn left and, later, right into Don Street to reach St Machar Drive. Cross this and go straight ahead into High Street. At the top sits the Old Town House, built in 1788/89. Continue down High Street.

Old Aberdeen is dominated by the university – the third oldest in Scotland. However, even older occupations are apparent from the street names such as Wrights' and Coopers' Place, where iron workers and barrel makers once lived and worked. To visit King's College, pass the impressive tomb of the university's founder, Bishop Elphinstone, and go through the arch. Continuing along High Street, pass an impressive turreted gateway before turning left onto University Road.

Bear right at King Street and cross at the traffic lights, turning left at Linksfield Road. A right turn at the end leads along Golf Road which passes Pittodrie, home of Aberdeen Football Club. As it curves onto Park Road, cross the road to climb the grassy mound ahead with good views over the beach and city. The path leads back down to the Beach Ballroom.

13

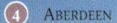

Torry Battery and Girdle Ness

Distance 3.75km **Time** 1 hour 30
Terrain city streets, coastal path, road with
pavement, steps **Map** OS Explorer 406
Access buses from Aberdeen city centre
to Torry

Only a short hop from the bright lights and
designer shops of Aberdeen's centre, the
headland of Girdle Ness has helped protect
Aberdeen's important harbour since
Napoleonic times. Explore the artillery
battery and lighthouse which command
extensive sea views, before returning
through a residential area of the city.

The walk starts from the Torry Battery car
park, situated off the road that loops around
Girdle Ness. It can be easily reached on foot
or by bus from the city centre by crossing
Victoria Bridge and then following the road
nearest to the shore past a number of fish
merchants before reaching the open ground
of Girdle Ness.

Defensive structures on this prominent
headland overlooking Aberdeen and its
harbour are thought to date back to the
1490s when the town's armoury was kept
here and the location allegedly used for the
execution of captured pirates. Fear of a
French invasion under Napoleon ensured
that more substantial emplacements and
fortifications were built here; the battery
was heavily used during the First World
War. During the inter-war years, the
barracks were used to temporarily house
homeless families until being declared
unfit for human habitation in 1938. The
Second World War saw Torry Battery
brought back into military use with the
installation of anti-aircraft guns and heavy
artillery. History repeated itself during the
housing crisis after the war when the
battery again became home to a number of
families, who continued to live there well
into the 1950s. Today, the Greyhope Bay

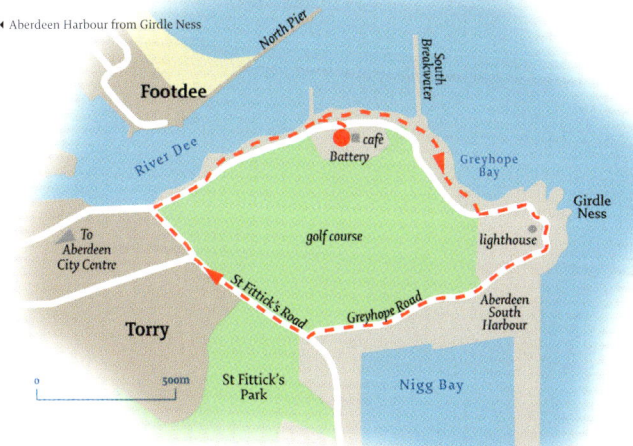

◀ Aberdeen Harbour from Girdle Ness

Footdee

North Pier

South Breakwater

café
Battery

Greyhope Bay

River Dee

Girdle Ness

To Aberdeen City Centre

golf course

lighthouse

St Fittick's Road

Greyhope Road

Aberdeen South Harbour

Torry

St Fittick's Park

Nigg Bay

0   500m

Centre at the Battery houses a café which is a great place to dolphin-watch from.

Start the walk by leaving the battery and heading down to the road. Turn left but very soon take a path on the right down steps to reach the shore. Keep right at the bottom to follow the coastline. The wide river mouth is popular with dolphins who seem unbothered by the international shipping trade – so keep your eyes peeled, especially during a running tide. Pass the blocked entrance to the South Breakwater which guards the harbour and has a white lighthouse at its far end. Climb the steps to reach a higher path which passes a car park and rejoins the road.

The road is now followed to the end of the headland and Girdle Ness Lighthouse. Prompted by the loss of 43 lives in the wrecking of an Aberdeen whaling boat, the lighthouse first shone in 1833 and stands 37m high. Originally powered by paraffin,

the light had 200,000 candlepower which could be seen 25 miles out to sea on a clear night. The elegant structure was damaged in 1944 when an unexploded mine drifted ashore and detonated nearby. Follow the road to pass the 'Torry Coo', a now redundant foghorn which, until 1987, sounded whenever visibility dropped below 8km.

Continue along the road overlooking South Harbour to reach a road junction. Turn right here to climb St Fittick's Road, which crosses the headland inland. When the main road bends left, keep straight ahead to descend back to the northern side. Bear right along the road and keep an eye out for a signed path heading down to the shore on the left. Follow this path back to the bottom of the steps near the start of the walk and climb these to return to the car park at the start.

Hazlehead Park

Distance 4.5km **Time** 1 hour 30
Terrain clear paths, muddy in winter
Map OS Explorer 406 **Access** buses from
Aberdeen city centre to Skene Road; walk
along Groats Road to the start

**Hazlehead Park and its woodlands by
Aberdeen's western suburbs has
something for everyone – formal gardens,
sculptures, forest paths, two golf courses,
a café and – for the children and young at
heart – a massive maze, a pets' corner and
a great play area. There is an admission
charge for the pets' corner.**

Hazlehead Park has a number of car
parks and is easily reached by bus from the
city centre. This walk is described from the
car park behind the café, located at the end
of the driveway from Groats Road, but the
other car parks will do as long as you find
the café as the start point. From the car
park, pass the toilets to reach the front of

the café. From here, turn right onto the
main path which heads west through the
park. At a crosspaths, it is worth making
short detours off to either side. The path
on the right leads past a granite sculpture
entitled *Archaic Form* to reach the maze.
Scotland's oldest, it was first planted in
1935 and remains a real challenge to adults
and children alike. If you really get lost, the
maze can be solved by placing one hand
against either wall and keeping it there
while walking forward although this takes
some of the fun away too.

On the other side of the main path is the
rose garden, home to a striking memorial
to the 167 men who lost their lives in the
Piper Alpha oil rig disaster in 1988.
Aberdeen owes its current prosperity to the
North Sea oil industry and this horrific
tragedy directly affected many in the area.
The adjacent garden is dedicated to the
Queen Mother and contains a lovely

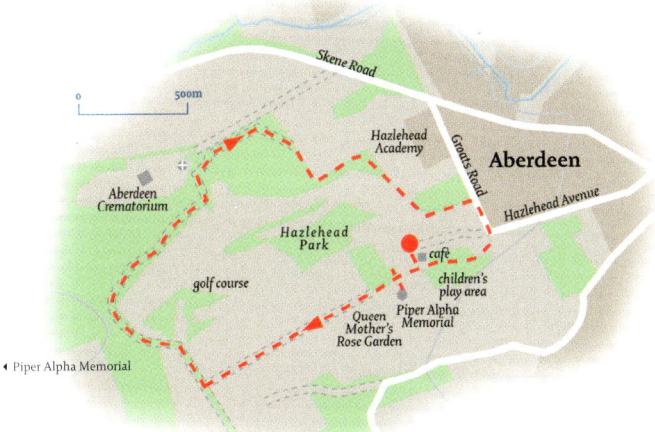

0   500m

Skene Road

Hazlehead
Academy

Aberdeen
Crematorium

Aberdeen

Groats Road

Hazlehead Avenue

Hazlehead
Park

café

golf course

children's
play area

Queen
Mother's
Rose Garden

Piper Alpha
Memorial

◄ Piper Alpha Memorial

sculpture of a woman and a dove. Return to the main path and continue to reach the edge of the formal part of the park. Pass through the gateway and cross the track, staying on the wide path between the golf courses – signed for Anderson Woods.

The park was once the estate of Hazlehead House, home of local shipbuilder, William Rose. Now owned by the city council, it was opened to the public in 1920 and is very popular with runners, horse riders and mountain bikers, as well as walkers and families. Turn right at the T-junction (signposted for Anderson Woods) and keep left at the next fork to pass a wooden shelter. At the next junction keep right – signposted for the Anderson and Hazlehead Wood Trail. The path meanders through varied woodland with Aberdeen Crematorium visible through the trees on the left.

The path swings left and, as it almost emerges on a track, keep right to remain amongst the trees. At the next junction, where there is a parallel track, keep straight on; both routes then join and bear left into mature beechwoods. In a while, the wide path runs alongside a playing field; keep left here before passing a small play area (a much bigger one is visited at the end of the walk).

At Groats Road, turn right; at the T-junction go straight ahead between the stone gateposts to return to the formal park area. Here the pets' corner can be visited to the right; otherwise follow the main path, bearing right through a conifer garden to reach a wide grassy expanse. At the far side, there is an impressively large children's play area. To return to the car park at the start, turn right just before the café building.

Duthie Park and the River Dee

Distance 11.5km **Time** 3 hours
Terrain park paths, rough riverside path
and cyclepath **Map** OS Explorer 406
Access regular buses from Aberdeen city
centre to Duthie Park

**Explore fabulous Duthie Park with its
acres of informal landscaping, Winter
Gardens and rose garden, before following
a rough anglers' path upstream. The return
is along the old Deeside railway line.
Note that this route can be impassable if
the river is in flood.**

The walk starts from the car park on the
southeastern edge of the park, near the
River Dee, but can be joined from any of
the entrances to the park. The 44-acre site
was donated to the city by Elizabeth
Crombie Duthie in 1880. At its centre is a
vast green space with a traditional
Victorian bandstand. It's also worth
visiting the David Welch Winter Gardens,
a series of glasshouses; the various zones

include an arid area with one of the UK's
largest collection of cacti, as well as
impressive tropical and temperate zones.
There's also a café and toilets.

From the car park, follow the path up
the rise between the slides and the
boating lake, then bear left to head past a
fountain, aiming directly for the obelisk.
Pass this and cross a bridge over the
ponds, leaving Duthie Park via the gates
at the southwest corner.

Aiming for the banks of the River Dee
on the far side of the roundabout, take the
pelican crossing directly ahead and then
cross over the very busy A945. From here,
a surfaced path slopes down to the river;
follow it upstream. The Dee is one of the
most celebrated of salmon rivers, rising
high on Braeriach in the Cairngorms and
running through some of the country's
finest scenery to reach here.

At the Bridge of Dee, leave the surfaced
path and pass under the nearest arch of

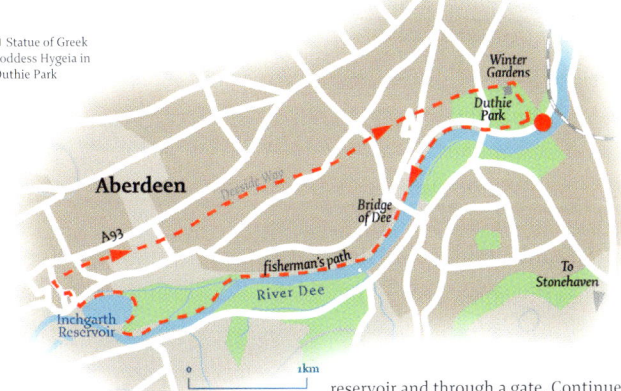

◀ Statue of Greek goddess Hygeia in Duthie Park

the bridge. Do not attempt this if the arch is flooded – at such times you will have to turn back. Follow the fishermen's path close to the water's edge. The going is rough and it can become overgrown in the summer but it sticks fairly close to the river, out of sight of the factories and warehouses above. Ignore steps off right that lead up to the university buildings. Eventually, the path climbs a few steps and then leads to a bridge over a tributary. After almost another 1km, pass under powerlines and then bear right away from the river, heading through a tunnel of broom.

As you emerge, keep to the right of the reservoir buildings and pass through a pedestrian gate onto a surfaced lane around Inchgarth Reservoir. Follow this round to the right and climb to a junction; keep right here, heading away from the

reservoir and through a gate. Continue ahead to a crossroads and go straight across, heading uphill onto Primrosehill Avenue. This curves to the left to reach a T-junction; turn right here. Ignore a path down to the left and continue on the road towards a high railway bridge.

Just before reaching this, take a path up on the left that climbs to reach the old railway line and turn right along this. The Deeside Line once ran up the strath as far as Ballater; a proposed extension to Braemar was thwarted by Queen Victoria's concerns about her privacy at Balmoral.

The level cycle route provides a pleasant 4km walk back to Duthie Park. Along the way it leads under three roadbridges and over two more, including the striking Holburn Bridge which was opened in 2004 as the old line was turned over to cyclists. At the end of the line, follow the path leading down to the right to the park gates and return to the start.

Tyrebagger Wood and Elrick Hill

Distance 4.25km **Time** 1 hour 30
Terrain clear paths, rough and muddy
underfoot in places **Map** OS Explorer 406
Access buses from Aberdeen and Inverurie
stop on the A96

This varied short walk combines a forest
trail with an exploration of the more open,
natural landscape of Elrick Hill. The name
Tyrebagger is thought to come from the
Gaelic *tir*, which means 'land', and *balgair*,
meaning 'fox', translating as 'the Land
of the Fox'.

Take the B979 leading south off the A96
to reach the walk start point at the first of
two Tyrebagger Forest Trails car parks. Set
off along the red waymarked path which
begins next to the information board and
stays close to the road before diving deeper
into the forest. At first, this route follows

the Robbers' Trail, named after a cave said
to have been used by 17th-century outlaws,
before detouring to include the moorland
and summit of Elrick Hill.

Keep left at a clear fork in the path,
ignoring the path to the right which leads
to the second car park. Ignore a blue
waymarked path on the left and keep
following the red markers. After a bench
take the signed path on the right and cross
a pair of bridges over an area of wet
ground. After this the path climbs gently
and as it approaches an old stone wall keep
left and soon afterwards turn right,
following a sign for the Circular Path.

The next stage of the walk delves into an
attractive landscape of heather dotted with
rowans and birches. At a fork, keep left to
stay on the main path. At the next fork you
can either take the smaller path on the

left to head directly up to the summit of Elrick Hill or continue to a crossroads of paths where a clearer path heads left to climb to the top.

The wooded summit of this conical hill has a number of benches and good views between the trees. Keep an eye out for the rare capercaillie, a large endangered member of the grouse family. The elusive birds tend to stay out of the way of humans so you'd be pretty lucky to spot one, but you might catch their distinctive clip-clop call which has earned them the nickname 'the horse of the woods'.

The hill is said to have been given to the city of Aberdeen by Robert the Bruce in the 14th century. Return to the crossroads of paths and continue on the circular path as it crosses the eastern flank of the hill. At the next path junction, bear right, following the sign for West Wood and Brimmond, and keep right again near a telegraph pole.

Cross a footbridge over a burn, turning left on the far bank to head through the woods. Keep right when a larger track is reached and turn right at the next junction. Keep left at a final junction to follow the path back to the Tyrebagger car park.

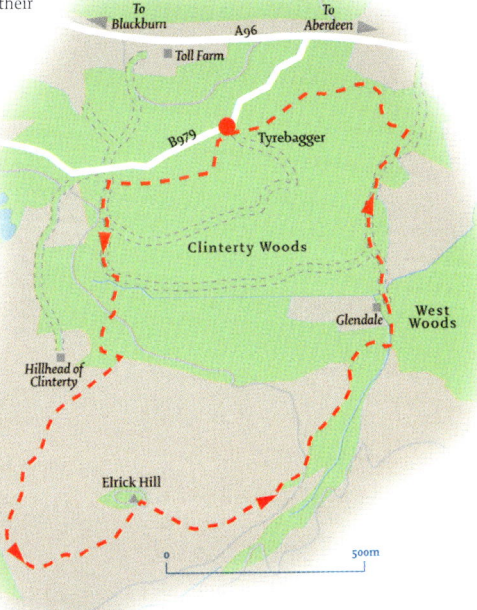

Kirkhill Forest and Tyrebagger Hill

Distance 6.75km **Time** 2 hours
Terrain waymarked paths and tracks,
muddy at times **Map** OS Explorer 406
Access buses from Aberdeen and Inverurie
stop on the A96

**Kirkhill Forest, just a few miles from the
fringes of Aberdeen, makes a great location
for this quiet leg stretcher, which climbs
to the top of Tyrebagger Hill and its
viewing tower.**

Kirkhill Forest is on the north side of the
A96, just west of Aberdeen Airport between
the Dyce roundabout and the Blackburn
roundabout; follow the track signed for
mountain bike trails to reach the car park.
There is also a permanent orienteering
course here – you can download the course
map from the Forestry and Land Scotland
website if you want to give it a go. Begin

the walk by heading through the gate at the
far end of the car park, and follow the track
beyond. Despite the close proximity of a
busy road and airport, the forest is
surprisingly peaceful – just watch out for
any mountain bikers. Keep on the track
when it curves right at a junction, now
following the white waymarkers.

Again, remain on the main track as it
turns right once more. After a long straight
section keep left at a fork. The track then
swings sharply to the left and right.
Continue following the white waymarkers,
passing through a gate, and turn left at
a T-junction.

Ignore the route back to the car park
and keep an eye out for a marker which
indicates a smaller path on the right.
It makes a change to leave the forestry
tracks behind; the path climbs up through

◄ The Tappie Tower

the trees before emerging on the open summit of Tyrebagger Hill. The Tappie Tower provides the final surprise – a small cylindrical stone viewing tower with a spiral stairway. Such towers are popular locally and this granite structure was erected in the 19th century by local landowner Dr William Henderson to mark the highest point on his estate. From the top, there are excellent views over the area, including Mither Tap on Bennachie.

The white waymarked trail turns back here to retrace the outward climb to the track, but to avoid going over the same ground continue on the rougher path ahead until it descends to a track and then turn left to follow this back around the hill to where you left the track on the ascent. Continue ahead, retracing your steps initially, but after 150m turn right onto a path leading through the trees. A wide view to the southwest soon opens up. Keep straight ahead at a junction, and stay on the main path when another leads off to the right. Eventually the path reaches a track once more; turn right here to rejoin the outward route back to the car park.

The coastline stretches away to the south of Aberdeen with craggy cliffs leading to the town of Stonehaven. Aberdeenshire is famed for its castles, but for spectacle none can rival Dunnottar, a massive fortress on a plug of rock surrounded by the crashing waves – accessed only by a thin ribbon of rock joining it to the main cliff. The whirling seabirds get the best view, but even from land Dunnottar is breathtaking enough to have become an icon of Scotland and a great focal point to a walk from the town.

Beyond Dunnottar, the coast sweeps onwards towards the border with Angus, dotted with old fishing villages and harbours such as Gourdon and Johnshaven. The grand finale to the Aberdeenshire coastline is the vast sandy beach below St Cyrus – the perfect spot to relax or explore the National Nature Reserve and remains of the salmon netting industry.

Stretching inland towards the Mounth hills is the fertile Howe of the Mearns, where rich farmland is fringed by gentle rolling hills. The harshness of rural life here in the early 1900s was immortalised in the works of Lewis Grassic Gibbon, and agriculture remains important today. Beyond the forested foothills, the massive granite tor on Clachnaben, on the edge of the vast empty Mounth Plateau, is an ever-popular objective for walkers.

Stonehaven and the Mearns

Stonehaven to Dunnottar Castle

Distance 5km **Time** 1 hour 30
Terrain waymarked path with steep climb,
minor road to return **Map** OS Explorer 396
Access buses and trains from Aberdeen
and Montrose to Stonehaven

There is no better way to reach the fortress
of Dunnottar Castle than this bracing
clifftop walk from Stonehaven Harbour.
Although Dunnottar Castle steals much of
the attention on this stretch of the
seaboard, Stonehaven has attractions of its
own and a lido dating back to the 1930s
graces the northern end of the seafront.

   This route begins from the other end of
Stonehaven, near the harbour and the 16th-
century Tolbooth. The fascinating building
was originally a storehouse, then a
courthouse and prison and now houses a
small museum as well as a restaurant. The
car park is behind the Tolbooth.

   To start the walk, turn right out of the car
park, passing the front of the Tolbooth,
and then turn left to cross the back of the
harbour. Keep a keen eye out for a footpath
sign on the right which leads you up
Wallace Wynd. Bear left past houses to
make the sharp climb on a surfaced path
which passes the steep back gardens of the
harbourside cottages, crossing land known
as the Bervie Braes. When this emerges at
the road, turn left and take in the views
back down over Stonehaven. At a small
parking area, leave the road to take the
clear footpath uphill between fences.

   At the top of the rise, the first glimpse of
Dunnottar Castle is revealed. Here, it is
worth making the short detour through
the gate on the right to climb to the large
war memorial atop Black Hill. The
memorial was deliberately designed to
look unfinished, testament to the ruined
lives which it commemorates. After
returning to the coast path, continue
towards Dunnottar.

   Follow the path as it weaves around

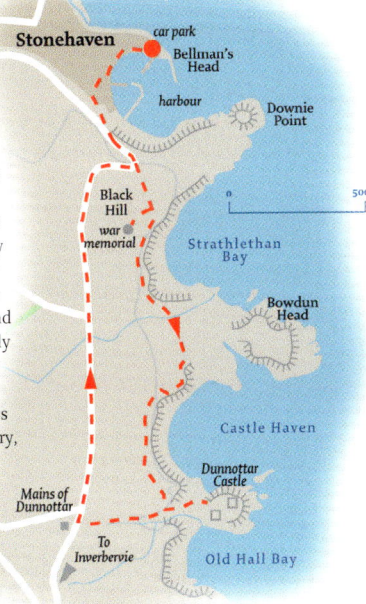

the back of Strathlethan Bay before bearing right at a sign to cut across the next headland. As you near the castle, a number of paths head out to a multitude of viewpoints. One of the best vantage points is from the top of the steps on the main route down to the castle. Owned by the Cowdray family, there is a charge for admission. It is well worth exploring the ruins for the chance to soak up its rich and bloody history. The extensive site actually houses 11 distinct buildings, dating from the 13th to 17th centuries, although it is thought that there has been a fortress here since Pictish times. In the 9th century, the castle was destroyed by the Vikings in a battle which also saw the death of King Donald II.

In 1650, Dunnottar provided refuge to Charles II soon after Cromwell had seized power in England. Following Charles' impromptu crowning at Scone, the Scottish crown jewels needed to be concealed as Edinburgh had fallen to Cromwell; they were taken to Dunnottar for safekeeping. This led to an eight-month siege of the castle, with 70 men holding out until ultimately defeated by the arrival of heavy cannon. Although the Scots surrendered, the crown jewels had been smuggled out of the castle to be buried under the floor of nearby Kinneff Church where they remained for the next 11 years.

Scotland continued to be gripped by unrest and, in 1685, there was a new group of prisoners at Dunnottar: 167 Covenanters spent two months in an almost airless cellar. A number took the oath of allegiance to the King, several died – some during escape attempts – but the majority were finally deported to the West Indies.

The most scenic return is back along the coast path. However, it is also possible to make a circular route by heading inland on the main path from the castle and turning right on the minor road. Follow the verge to reach the outskirts of Stonehaven and pick up the steps down the Bervie Braes to return to the start.

◀ Overlooking Stonehaven

27

Inverbervie to Johnshaven

Distance 7.5km **Time** 2 hours (one way)
Terrain easy, level walking
Maps OS Explorer 382 and 396 **Access** buses
from Aberdeen and Montrose stop at
Inverbervie and Johnshaven

This walk traces the coastline south from
Inverbervie to visit Gourdon Harbour
before continuing to the old fishing village
of Johnshaven. A bus can be used for
the return.

   Start from the square just off the main
street at the northern end of Inverbervie.
There is parking here, as well as the bus
stop and ancient mercat cross marking the
traditional market and meeting point.
Head past the cross and along High Street
before turning right at the bottom onto
David Street and then left at the crossroads
towards the seafront. Starting out as a

small fishing village, Inverbervie's fortunes
changed with the growth of the textile
industry during the Industrial Revolution.
At one point there were nine flax spinning
mills here, employing more than 500
people. Later, life in this corner of Scotland
was immortalised in the works of Lewis
Grassic Gibbon who was brought up in
nearby Arbuthnott. *Sunset Song* was his first
and best known novel, the story
of a young woman enduring a tough
upbringing and life on a Mearns farm at
the turn of the century.

   Before reaching the seafront, aim right
on a surfaced cycleway with houses on
your right and grass to the left. Keep
following this shared path as it runs along
the coast (alternatively there is a path
nearer the sea, although this can be
muddy in places). When the houses of

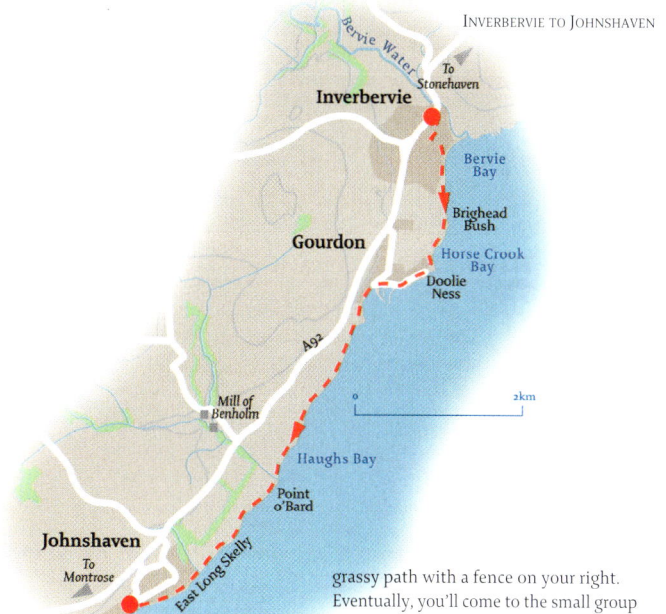

Gourdon come into view, turn left onto a rough path just before a metal shed on the right. Follow this to reach a surfaced road through the streets of the fishing village. The older of the two harbours seen today was the work of Thomas Telford, built in 1819, with the more modern one added in 1859 to cope with the demands of the herring boom when more than 8000 barrels of the fish were exported annually from Gourdon at its height.

Pass the Maggie Law Maritime Museum and harbours, and continue ahead on the track behind the Harbour Bar. After the last house the track narrows to a wide grassy path with a fence on your right. Eventually, you'll come to the small group of houses at the Haughs of Benholm. Keep following the track which runs between a drystane dyke on your right and the sea. Walk past an entrance to a school and a vehicle barrier before passing Wairds Park caravan park to reach Johnshaven. Boats parked up like cars and the piles of creel pots around the harbour show that fishing remains an important part of life here.

The village hosts the very popular Fish Festival in early August when the harbour is crammed with stalls, cooking demonstrations, live music and a lot of people messing about in boats. At the harbour, turn right to pass The Anchor Hotel where the bus stop is located opposite for the return trip to Inverbervie.

◀ Gourdon Harbour

St Cyrus beach and cliff circuit

Distance 5km **Time** 1 hour 15
Terrain sandy beach, steep cliff paths
Map OS Explorer 382 **Access** buses from
Aberdeen and Montrose to St Cyrus village

**Head out along the fine sand of St Cyrus
beach before climbing the cliffs for
spectacular views. Return past old salmon
bothies through the National Nature
Reserve. The walk can also be started from
St Cyrus village.**

Start from the St Cyrus National Nature
Reserve Visitor Centre, housed in an old
lifeboat station, 6km north of Montrose off
the A92. The visitor centre is open daily
from April to October and Monday to
Friday from November to March. For those
using the bus, it is also possible to start the
walk from St Cyrus – follow Beach Road
past the church to the clifftop car park
where the circuit can be picked up.

Begin by taking the roadside path from
the old lifeboat station towards the
cottages which housed salmon fishermen
until the 1990s. The path passes in front of
the building, and the turf roof of the old
icehouse can be seen beyond. This was
once used to store the ice to pack the fish,
but has been converted into a stylish
home. Turn right to cross the long wooden
bridge spanning the old riverbed of the
North Esk. Water flowed here until an epic
storm in 1879 when floodwaters raging
down the river combined with stormy seas
to beach the dunes 1.5km further south
where a new river mouth was formed. The
reedbeds now provide a fertile habitat for a
variety of birds and insects.

Climb the path over the dunes and down
onto the wide sandy beach. Montrose can
be seen to the south, whilst the high cliffs
make a spectacular backdrop. These cliffs,

◄ St Cyrus seafront

set well back from and above the beach, are testament to the changing sea levels at the end of the last ice age. The face weathers over time, depositing minerals on the grasslands below, resulting in the diverse habitat of rare plant species. One plant to look out for at this stage in the walk is purple-flowering sea rocket which survives in the border between dune and beach.

Turn left along the beach, aiming for the prominent low white clifftop cottage and, once below it, climb the steep path up the cliff. The path passes an icehouse at the top; turn left a little further up to pass the buildings at Woodston and turn left again onto the grassy cliff path, which has stunning views down the coast.

After a short while, you come to the car park near St Cyrus village. Here, take the steep path back down the cliff, keeping an eye out for peregrine falcons that make this their home. Turn right at the bottom to pass the old salmon bothies used for the commercial salmon netting industry which only died out completely in 2007. At a fork, keep left to return to the bridge and the start of the walk. However, you may want to detour straight ahead to visit Nether Kirkyard.

Dating back to 1242, it contains many interesting memorials, including the grave of George Beattie, a local poet who shot himself here in 1823 after being jilted in favour of a wealthier man. Look out for the watch hut in the corner where relatives of the recently deceased would have kept watch overnight to thwart bodysnatchers in the nights after a burial.

Kerloch

Distance 10km **Time** 3 hours 30
Terrain forestry tracks (rough and stony in
places) almost to the top, short section of
moorland path **Map** OS Explorer 396
Access no public transport to the start

**This reasonably easy hillwalk reaches the
remote summit of Kerloch which rewards
with far-reaching views over the
surrounding countryside.**

To reach the start turn east off the B974
just south of Strachan, which lies to the
southwest of Banchory. Follow this minor
road for around 3km – if you encounter
Knockburn Loch Activity Centre you've
come too far. Just opposite the turn-off for
Wester Knockhill Cottage, look out for a
track, signposted as a public footpath to
Glenbervie by the Stockmounth, which
leads south. There is a small parking area
at the start of the track.

Begin by walking along the track, the
route of an ancient road for drovers
heading to the market at Laurencekirk.
The hill of Kerloch can be seen ahead as
the route crosses grazing land. Go straight
on at two gates before you reach the edge
of the forestry plantation. Continue on
the track as it starts to climb alongside a
more open area with good views of the
surrounding countryside and past a
small private cabin.

At a fork in the track take the smaller
route on the right-hand side to climb more
steeply through the trees. The track is
stony and eroded underfoot in places but
zigzags to gain height a little more gently
than heading straight for the summit.
Looking back, the Hill of Fare can be seen
in the distance. Eventually the route
emerges from the trees and the track
continues heading uphill across heather

moorland. This can be a good place to look out for birds of prey, including buzzard, merlin and osprey in the summer months.

As you get closer to the summit, watch out for a path which forks right to head directly to the cairn marking the summit and the trig point just a little further beyond. From here there is an expansive view with the rocky tor of Clachnaben clearly visible while in the distance the distinctive shape of Mither Tap, the site of

an historic hillfort, can also be made out.

From the top the quickest and easiest way back is simply to retrace the outward route down the path and track to the road. If you have a map and prefer a more challenging route it is possible to head west to the slightly smaller summit of Little Kerloch and then aim northwest to Melmannoch to pick up a forestry track which leads eventually to Pitreadie Farm and back to the minor road a little west of your start point.

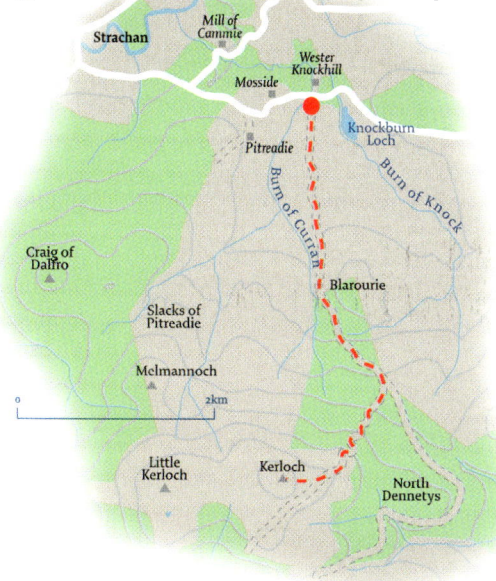

Clachnaben

Distance 9km **Time** 3 hours
Terrain tracks, then good hill path; boggy
sections **Maps** OS Explorer OL54 and 396
Access no public transport to the start

**The spectacular granite tor at the top of
Clachnaben makes it one of the most
distinctive landmarks in the region.
A closer acquaintance doesn't disappoint,
as in clear weather this fine hill offers
superb 360-degree views.**

The route begins from the forest car park
situated in an old quarry 750m north of the
Bridge of Dye on the Cairn o'Mount road
between Banchory and Fettercairn. Follow
the path as it heads southwest, running
almost parallel to the road at first, and
then continuing through the forestry. On
reaching open ground, go straight on to
cross a track and follow the route alongside
the stone wall ahead. Slightly alarmingly

for a hill walk, the start is mostly downhill.

Climb the stile beside a gate and
continue down to the bottom of the glen,
where the track crosses a bridge. Take the
right fork on the far side to follow the track
which heads up through Miller's Bog,
staying on the main route when smaller
tracks branch off. At a clear fork, keep right
to continue along the glen floor, crossing
footbridges over several small burns. The
massive tor on top of Clachnaben –
actually a granite plug, the remains from
a long-extinct volcano – can be clearly seen
ahead. From here, it is easy to see how it
got its name from the Gaelic *Clach na
Beinne*, 'the Stone on the Hill'. As it
continues, the path keeps mainly to the
left edge of the trees above the fast-flowing
Mill Burn.

At the top of the plantation, the terrain
changes to moorland. The path climbs up a

◄ Heading for Clachnaben

section of pitched stone steps, aiming well to the right of Clachnaben and overlooking the steep-sided Slack of Dye. The great size of the tor can be appreciated on the final stretch of the approach, and you may well see climbers attempting the many climbing and bouldering routes on its front face. However, the path passes to the right to reach the gentler side of the tor. Reaching the very top requires a scramble, though great care is needed as the summit is tiny and surrounded by significant drops.

The superb summit view takes in much of Aberdeenshire, including Mither Tap on Bennachie to the north, as well as Mount Battock and Lochnagar to the west. There are a number of possible variants on the descent, though none with as good a view as the outward route and it is best to retrace your ascent to avoid undue erosion.

If heading for Clachnaben in April, you may well find yourself amidst runners taking part in the annual hill race. The gruelling 13.6km circuit takes in nearby Mount Shade and Threestane Hill and there is often snow still lying on the heathery ground to provide a further impediment to those aiming to beat the present record finishing time of just over one hour.

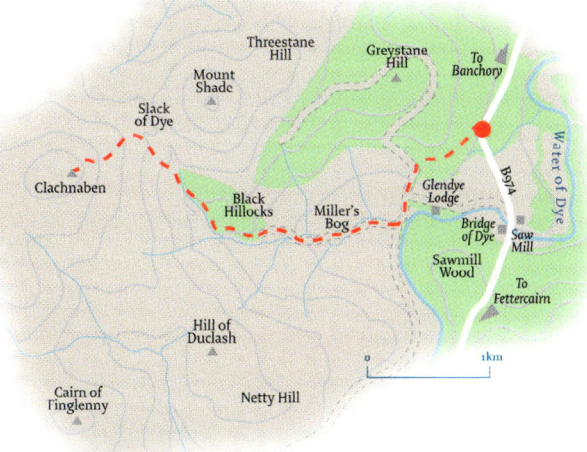

35

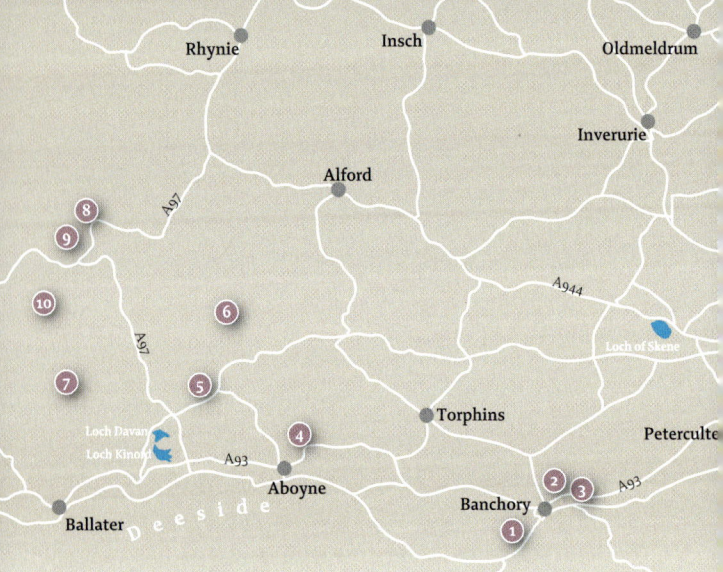

With its majestic salmon rivers, stately castles, rolling farmland and ancient pinewoods, this is the quintessential Aberdeenshire landscape. Whilst the glories of Deeside are widely known, upper Strathdon and, in particular, the area around Glenbuchat can seem deserted even in high summer. There is every opportunity to get away from it all with moorland walks over springy heather and plenty of delightful small hills offering panoramic views.

If castles and gardens are your thing, you cannot afford to miss Crathes, just east of Banchory. Here the immaculately tended walled flower gardens with their immense yew topiary hedgerows are amongst the most celebrated in Scotland. The turrets of the fine towerhouse castle provide the

prefect backdrop. There is a great walk around the expansive estate grounds here, whilst another walk traces the mighty Dee from Banchory to visit the castle.

Neighbouring Cromar and Strathdon remain primarily agricultural and forestry areas, although tourism is becoming increasingly important here too. This comparatively remote area well rewards the effort of seeking it out – though do remember your map.

Like much of North East Scotland, the area is rich in prehistoric remains, including cists, stone circles and souterrains. In the Howe of Cromar, Tomnaverie is a fine example of a recumbent stone circle that some archaeologists believe may have helped farmers record the seasons 3000 years ago.

Descent to Glen Buchat ▶

Deeside and Upper Donside

Scolty Hill

Distance 3.25km **Time** 1 hour
Terrain waymarked, clear path, steep
in places **Map** OS Explorer 406
Access buses from Aberdeen and
Braemar to Banchory

**Scolty Hill is a familiar feature in the
Banchory landscape, topped by a stone
tower where a climb up the spiral staircase
enables you to test your head for heights.
This is a perfect spot to drink in a sunset
over the Cairngorms.**

Scolty Woodlands are 1.5km south of
Banchory and this walk can easily be
extended by walking to the forest car park
at the start – a further detour would allow
an exploration of the Falls of Feugh and its
popular restaurant. From Banchory, take

the B974 south and once over the Dee take
the first right and follow the signs to reach
the car park.

The woods are often busy with a mix
of dog walkers, mountain bikers,
orienteers and runners. From the car park
head up to the main track going west,
ignoring the red and yellow markers. Keep
straight on when the Deeside Way track
heads right, and ahead again when the
main track turns left. The track climbs
gently to reach a wooden gate; go through
this and bear left. Soon take a marked
path on the right to head more steeply
uphill. The climb is fairly strenuous but
short and rewarded with great views
down to Banchory and over Deeside.

Scolty Tower soon looms into view.

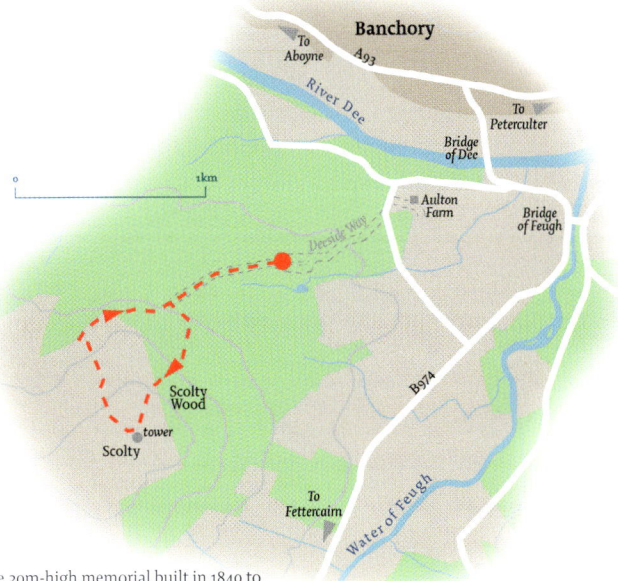

The 20m-high memorial built in 1840 to commemorate local landowner General William Burnett, a Royal Navy surgeon who served under the Duke of Wellington and took part in the Battle of Trafalgar, has been restored a number of times and now contains a robust metal spiral staircase allowing the climb to the top. The blast of wind you receive as you emerge into the wire viewing cage will take your breath away even if the panorama does not. To the east, Aberdeen and the coastline can be seen on a clear day, whilst looking towards the Cairngorms, Mount Keen and Morven are the most prominent summits. The large rocky tor crowning Clachnaben is easy to identify to the southwest.

From the base of the tower head slightly west, immediately forking right from the main ridge route to follow a path downhill, with good views over Banchory Hill. The mixed woodland on the descent supports a dense undergrowth of blaeberries, heather and other plants. Blaeberries are packed with vitamin C and flavour – you can't keep a taste for them a secret as they stain your mouth purple.

When the path comes out on a larger route turn right. This soon returns to the junction with the wooden gate; go straight ahead through this and follow the track back to the car park.

◀ Scolty Hill Tower

Banchory to Crathes Castle

Distance **8.25km** Time **2 hours (one way)**
Terrain **riverside paths and cyclepath**
Map **OS Explorer 406** Access **buses
from Milton of Crathes to Banchory for
the return**

Follow the course of the mighty River Dee
as it rushes towards the ocean from
Banchory. The courtyard at Milton of
Crathes can provide a spot of refreshment
or retail therapy before detouring to
fairytale Crathes Castle and then catching
the bus back.

There is a convenient car park (Bellfield)
on the east side of Dee Street in the centre
of Banchory. Start the walk by turning left
down Dee Street towards the river. Turn
left onto the lane that runs past the King
George V Park and Pavilion with
recreation fields on the right and a park
on the left. At the T-junction, dogleg left,
then second right onto a path which

heads under a box girder bridge and
emerges in a housing estate. Bear right to
follow the path curving round the back of
the houses and then through a parking
area. Further on, some steps on the right
descend to reach the riverside walkway
and the walk continues alongside the Dee.

In a while, the surfaced path leads to
the left away from the river to reach the
line of the old Royal Deeside Railway.
This is now a cycleway – turn right along
it, passing to the left of a fishing hut in
due course. Much of the old railway line
forms part of the Deeside Way, a walking
and cycling route linking Duthie Park in
Aberdeen with Ballater. After the fishing
hut, there is the option of taking a
rougher path closer to the river, but you
do have to return to the cycleway when
you reach a burn.

After emerging from the woods, the
cycleway reaches an open field and

◄ Crathes Castle

another riverbank option can be taken to the right until you reach the buildings at Birkenbaud, which you go around via the track to the left. Once past the buildings, either stay on the railway line or take the track back to the river to pass another fishing hut. If following the riverbank, go through the gate and at the far end of the field dogleg left to get into the next field, where you bear left to rejoin the cycleway just before Milton of Crathes. Here, part of the track has been restored and it is hoped that vintage trains will one day run to Banchory, which would make an excellent return option. For now, however, the track to the left heads up to the main road where there is a bus shelter for the trip back to town.

To detour to Crathes Castle before taking the bus, turn right through the courtyard and take the path to the left on the far side, which passes under the A93 onto the castle driveway. Once through the gates, a path on the left – waymarked in white – leads to the impressive fairytale castle, complete with turrets, and spectacular walled gardens known for their topiary and summer borders.

The original tower dates from the 16th century and its fascinating painted ceilings were restored in 2022. It is owned by the National Trust for Scotland and there is an admission charge to visit the castle and walled gardens; however, it is possible to view the castle from the outside and explore the parkland free of charge. Retrace the outward route as far as the craft village to reach the bus stop for the return to Banchory.

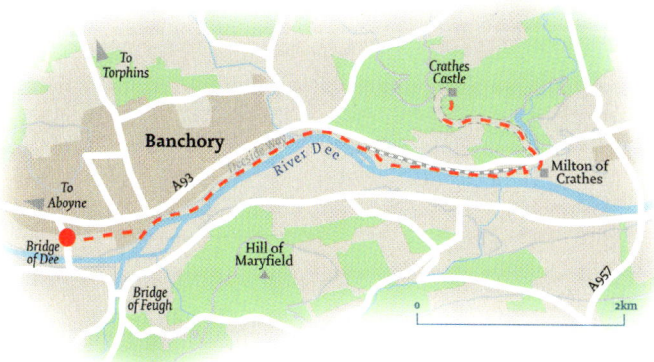

Ley Way and Crathes Castle

Distance 6.75km **Time** 2 hours
Terrain waymarked path through varied
woodland, park and farmland, rough in
places, passes an excellent children's play
area **Map** OS Explorer 406 **Access** buses
from Banchory and Aberdeen to Milton
of Crathes

A visit to Crathes Castle is a must as
this 16th-century towerhouse has a real
atmosphere as well as stunning walled
gardens. You can easily imagine a
bejewelled princess at an upper window
scanning the parkland for the approach of
her Prince Charming.

  Just east of Banchory off the A93, the
National Trust for Scotland's Crathes
Castle is a firm favourite with garden
lovers and those following the
Aberdeenshire Castle Trail. The land on
which it stands was originally given to the
Burnett family in the 1320s by Robert the
Bruce, although building work on the
towerhouse did not start until the mid-

1500s. Renowned for its painted ceilings,
the ghost which is said to haunt the
Green Lady's room, and the amazing
flowers and topiary in the walled garden,
Crathes can get very busy on sunny
afternoons. This is when the Ley Way,
leading through the extensive grounds
and taking in the less formal parkland,
woodland and farmland of the estate,
comes into its own. Although entry to the
parkland is free, there is a charge for
parking and for entry to the castle and
walled gardens.

  Start the walk from the visitor entrance
at the front of the castle, looking out on
the wide expanse of lawn. Take the main
path on the right-hand side of the grassy
area, opposite the walled gardens. At a
fork, bear right, following the red
waymarker. Just before the trees, there's a
pine marten sculpture; turn left here to
head up into the woodland, soon
branching right onto a narrower path and
then heading up steps next to a large rock

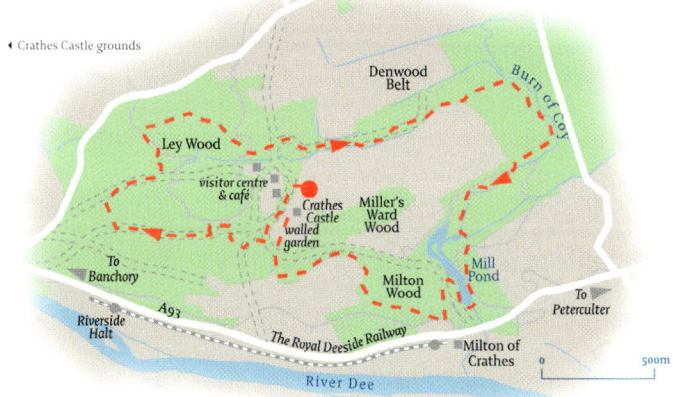

◄ Crathes Castle grounds

Denwood Belt

Burn of Coy

Ley Wood

visitor centre & café

Crathes Castle walled garden

Miller's Ward Wood

To Banchory

A93

Mill Pond

Milton Wood

To Peterculter

Riverside Halt

The Royal Deeside Railway

Milton of Crathes

0   500m

River Dee

wall with trees growing out of it. Head straight across the driveway to the castle and enter an area known as Caroline's Garden. Stay on the main path to pass a bench; eventually the path bears left.

When you reach a track, turn right along it, then right again (before reaching a bench) onto a woodland path, keeping a sharp eye on the markers as the route meanders through the trees. Turn right at a track and then left at an impressive Japanese fir. After some distance, cross a surfaced track and pass the play area.

Bear left here along a track, then branch right onto a waymarked path and keep to the markers as the trail switches between woodland and open fields before plunging again into the trees, following a path just to the right of a burn. Steps lead down to a lovely section of boardwalk where you can enjoy the damp habitat without having to squelch through the mud. Wood anemones and sorrel abound,

but keep an eye up to the branches too – you may catch a glimpse of a woodpecker, more often heard than seen.

Turn left to cross a bridge over the Coy Burn and, at the next junction, keep left again – the path to the right is a shortcut back to the castle. Another boardwalk and dense woodland lead to the mill pond. At the far end of the pond, turn right to cross a bridge over the outflow, passing the fish ladder that allows fish to continue their journey upstream beyond the otherwise insurmountable dam.

Keep following the red markers along the far side of the pond, heading up through the trees and across the castle driveway further on. Carry on along a meandering path which in a while leads down and then up a couple of short flights of steps. Eventually it meets a wider path which passes the estate cemetery to return to the front of Crathes Castle.

Mortlich circuit from Aboyne

Distance 10.25km **Time** 3 hours 30
Terrain pavement, golf course, woodland
paths, steep climb **Map** OS Explorer OL59
Access buses from Aberdeen, Banchory
and Braemar to Aboyne

**The crumbling remains of a hillfort sit
atop this little summit in the heart of
Deeside. The walk passes through varied
landscapes, including Aboyne golf course
and the Loch of Aboyne, before the steep
climb to the top. The return gives views to
the 13th-century Aboyne Castle, which
remains a private home.**

Aboyne is a lovely town set close by the
River Dee, about halfway between the
mountains and the sea. As well as the
famous salmon river and attractive
buildings, Aboyne has a couple of
excellent cafés. Start from the car park
outside the row of shops just off the main
road. First, cross the A93 towards the
public toilets and turn right along the

pavement, passing the entrance to
Aboyne Castle and crossing the Tarland
Burn. Keep left onto a residential road
which runs parallel to the A93.

Take the next left onto Golf Road which
unsurprisingly leads to the golf course.
Keep straight ahead when the main road
bends right towards houses, then ahead
again when the tarmac lane bends right
towards the clubhouse. When the track
forks, follow the main track which bears
right across the golf course towards the
loch, then curves left to lead close to the
shore. Keep right at a fork by a large pine
to cross a stile. After a short distance,
turn left onto a lovely path that leaves the
loch and winds up through the trees; it's a
little boggy in one or two places.

Eventually the path turns left when
there are broken bits of fence ahead.
Continue along the path to a conifer
plantation; here it turns right, soon
reaching a kissing gate. Pass through and

◀ Loch of Aboyne

continue to a T-junction. You'll return here on the descent, but for now turn right. Follow the path uphill, with the forest on your left, and enjoy the views over Deeside as you gain height. Go through a gate to continue the uphill climb, now steeply through the trees. The large summit cairn is seen across a broken-down fence. This is the site of a Pictish fort; a carved stone records that the cairn was erected for the 10th Marquis of Huntly who died in 1863.

Retrace your steps back down to the junction mentioned previously. Ignore the outward path (which is left) and instead go straight ahead through a gate. Continue through the trees to meet a forest track, then turn left. At the next junction, keep ahead. The route descends with views to Morven up ahead. When the main track swings right, go straight on, then turn left, cutting a corner. Continue along the track, which eventually becomes a path and curves right, descending to reach a footbridge.

Cross the bridge and continue up to the road. Cross and take the path opposite, which bears left and winds through the woods. When it meets a track, turn left along it, continuing down to housing on the edge of Aboyne. Turn left here, crossing the road and going through the gateway into the Aboyne Castle grounds opposite. A tarmac lane leads through an avenue of trees. Keep ahead at a crossroads (the Coos' Cathedral wedding venue is seen off left). Further on, there are views to 13th-century Aboyne Castle over to the left. Pass through a gateway and then turn right, following the lane beside the burn. This re-emerges on the A93; the starting car park is just to the right.

45

Tomnaverie and Drummy Wood

Distance 5km **Time** 1 hour 30
Terrain waymarked path, sometimes
overgrown **Map** OS Explorer OL59
Access buses from Aboyne and
Banchory to Tarland

**Feel the great sweep of time at the ancient
Tomnaverie Stone Circle on this delightful
walk from the quiet village of Tarland,
before returning through Drummy Wood.**

Start from Tarland square where the war
memorial is surrounded by attractive
stone-built shops, houses and two hotels.
Set in the middle of a large bowl of
agricultural land known as the Howe of
Cromar, the area is off the regular tourist
trail and is a real hidden gem.

The walk begins from the east end of
the square where it meets the main B9119;
an information board here has details of
this and other local walks. Turn right onto

Bridge Street. Once across the far side of
the river, look for a stone sculpture at the
start of a path running parallel to the road
on the left. The path bears left around a
house and then crosses a footbridge.
When it meets another road go straight
across, taking the path which continues
on the far side, again running parallel to
the road. Once over a stile, the path bears
right and crosses a track as it climbs up
to the stone circle.

Tomnaverie, erected about 4000 years
ago, is one of many recumbent circles in
this part of Scotland – a style found only
here and in Southwest Ireland. So named
because the largest stone is placed lying
down rather than standing, with two
large standing stones flanking it, the
purpose of these circles remains an
archaeological puzzle. They certainly have
some connections to the moon and

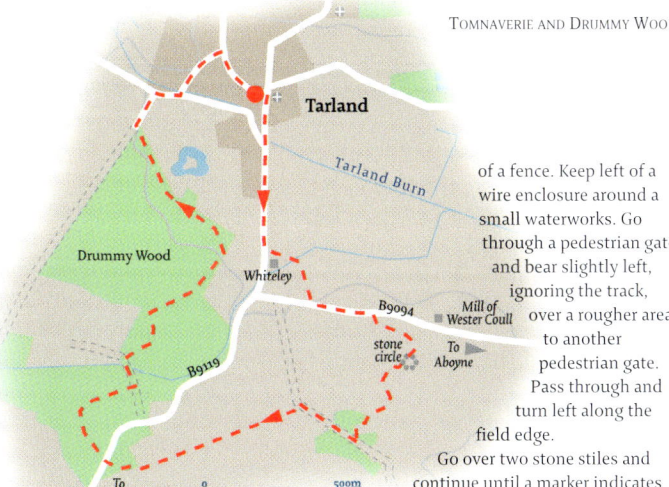

Tarland

Tarland Burn

Drummy Wood

Whiteley

B9094

Mill of
Wester Coull

stone
circle

To
Aboyne

B9119

To
Ballater

0   500m

of a fence. Keep left of a wire enclosure around a small waterworks. Go through a pedestrian gate and bear slightly left, ignoring the track, over a rougher area to another pedestrian gate. Pass through and turn left along the field edge.

Go over two stone stiles and continue until a marker indicates where to head left through the scattered trees. Cross over the remains of a wall and keep right along a good path once more, passing through another wall. Follow the path, crossing a stile to reach a track. Turn right and, when the track bends right, go through a kissing gate and bear left in the field, passing through another gate onto an enclosed path. Follow this until the path eventually bears right into a wood and then emerges on a minor road. Cross over and go through a gate leading to Drummy Wood.

At a track junction, bear right and then left for 100m before turning right to follow a path. When this reaches a clearing, curve left. The path runs along the edge of the wood before emerging at a car park. Follow the access track to Burnside Road, turning right onto this, then left along Mill Road to the garage. Go right to return to the square.

changing seasons, and are usually found on top of small hills amidst good farmland. This has led to speculation that they were used by farmers to plot the seasons by making lunar observations. Tomnaverie consists of 11 stones (there were 13 originally), four of which are still standing. The whole site is perched precariously on the edge of an old quarry – the steep drops are protected by a fence, but the stone circle came close to being swallowed up by the quarry when two stones were removed before intervention to protect the site in the 1920s.

The circle enjoys a glorious location with wide views taking in Morven, Clachnaben and the cairn-covered Balnagowan Hill, with Lochnagar in the far distance. Just beyond the stones, a waymarked path leads along the left side

◀ Tomnaverie Stone Circle

47

Pressendye

Distance 14km **Time** 4 hours
Terrain minor roads, tracks, hill path to exposed summit, some waymarking
Map OS Explorer OL59 **Access** buses from Aboyne and Banchory to Tarland

This varied circuit from the village of Tarland climbs up through farmland to the prominent hill of Pressendye before descending back through the woods.

The walk starts from the square in Tarland. Head west from here, keeping right past the war memorial. Follow the road as it curves right, ignoring the road off left at the garage. At the next junction go straight across onto a track leading to a small wetland area. Bear left at a fork and then left on the path to re-emerge on the minor road. Now turn right and follow the tarmac through open farmland.

Tarland is at the heart of the Howe of Cromar, a large hollow of land just outside the Cairngorms National Park. Numerous stone circles and other ancient artefacts litter the countryside here, providing evidence of the rich layers of human occupation over the centuries.

The road heads northwest; ignore the next turning on the right before bearing right at a clear fork. Continue past West Davoch and at the right-hand bend just after Easter Davoch, leave the surfaced road and go straight on up a track signed for Boultenstone.

Pass through the gate and follow this track uphill for 650m. At a track junction, turn right through a gate and continue by the fence. After 250m, turn left through a small gate and follow the path through the trees. Keep ahead at the end of the fence and at a further crosspaths before turning right at a marker post. The path soon reaches open moorland with views back towards Lochnagar and Morven.

At the ridge, go right onto a clearer track by a fence. As the track climbs over Broom

◀ Trees near Tarland

Hill, the views open up, with Pressendye visible beyond a dip, and easy ground underfoot. Stay by the fence, passing a small lochan in the dip. After this, near a gate, the path veers to the right a little in the trees, soon meeting another track; bear left up this to head back to the fence towards the summit. Just before the top, pass through a gate and continue by a broken-down old fence to the summit of Pressendye, marked with a trig point and an old cairn.

Take the waymarked track southeast, soon coming alongside a fence. Keep straight across at a mountain bike trail, then left when a track joins from the right, now amongst pines. At the next fork, bear right. Ignore a path off into the trees, keeping ahead on the track as it curves right. Where there is a picnic bench, turn right onto a smaller track downhill. Follow this as it leaves the trees and continues down through heather. At a junction, bear left, following the blue and red markers (ignoring the red-marked path off right). Cross another mountain bike trail and turn right at a bigger track. At the next junction, bear left downhill. After bending right, watch out for an easily missed turn to the right onto a lesser track which climbs beside the pylons.

Curve left to follow the track alongside mature beech trees with forestry on your left. At a grassy track, keep straight ahead onto a narrower path (diverging right from the track), following the waymarkers. On reaching a metal gate, turn right over the stile to follow a lovely path lined by beech trees. After crossing the burn, carry straight on, ignoring the red route off left. Turn left at a minor road; when the road bends left keep straight ahead on a grassy track with a hall and modern housing on the left. At the road, turn right, then left, keeping ahead to the centre of Tarland.

49

Morven

Distance 8.5km **Time** 4 hours 30
Terrain steep hill paths with boggy
sections **Map** OS Explorer OL59
Access no public transport to the start

Rural Aberdeenshire is dotted with hills
providing panoramic views – Morven is
one of the biggest and best, on the fringes
of the Cairngorms. Topped by an
enormous cairn, it is the toughest walk in
this guide, calling for hillwalking gear and
navigational skills, but it is well worth the
extra effort.

The start is on the minor road which
branches west from the A97, 1km south of
Logie Coldstone, signed for Groddie.
Where it forks at the end of the public
road, there is a small parking area. The
walk starts out along the left-hand fork,
but immediately turns left through a gate.

Climb through the field towards the
abandoned farmhouse of Balhennie,
passing through another gate to reach the
ruin. Pass to the left of it and then go
through the right of two adjacent gates.

Head up the field, keeping the fence on
your left to reach another gate and the
open moorland beyond. Two paths aim
for Morven from here – a steep and direct
route and an older path which makes
more gradual progress and is the return
option for this route. After the gate, bear
right along a grassy path which quickly
becomes clearer underfoot as it ascends
west up the steep slope, passing a
smattering of huge boulders and saplings
as it climbs. A break from the steep pull
gives a chance to appreciate the view over
the Cromar farmland below.

At around 600m, the gradient eases as a

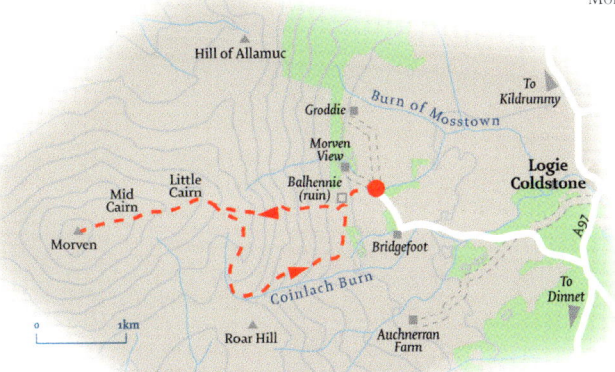

small shoulder is reached. Often wet underfoot, this is soon crossed and the route steepens again to reach a point just left of the rocky outcrop at Little Cairn. The path now climbs gradually, passing to the left of a second outcrop of rocks, Mid Cairn, to reveal the summit ahead for the first time. Cross the dip to reach the massive cairn and windshelter. The trig point can be found in a second shelter on the north side. The cairn itself is thought to date back to ancient times, although its purpose remains unclear. From here, the views are widespread; the distinctive shapes of Bennachie and Mither Tap are easy to pick out, as well as the granite tor of Clachnaben. To the south, the peak rising high above the moors is Mount Keen, whilst the fine northeastern corrie of Lochnagar can be seen further west.

The quickest way back is to retrace your steps, but there is a variant which is easier on your knees. Return past Mid and Little Cairn, but on the slope leading down to the flat 600m shoulder take a path which

forks slightly to the right, aiming for a bare patch in the heather and crossing a briefly boggy section. From here, vehicle tracks in the heather lead away south down to the bealach north of Roar Hill.

Bear left on a very faint grassy path that continues close to the burn. There's some boggy ground before the grass gives way to heather again and the path becomes clear. It now begins to descend northeast across the slope. Soon the path forks; the left branch is the old stalkers' route shown on maps but it is very overgrown lower down, so instead follow the clearer right branch. Rough at first, it later becomes a smooth grassy track. After a gate, continue downhill, but fork left onto a fainter ATV track well before reaching the woods. This grassy track leads north, crossing a short boggy area before reaching a gate at the north end of the plantation. Go through this and follow the track as it swings left to head back to the ruin at Balhennie. Retrace your steps to the start.

◀ Abandoned farmhouse at Balhennie

Glenbuchat Castle and ridge

Distance 16.7km **Time** 4-5 hours
Terrain hill tracks – optional detour to
summit across pathless heather
Map OS Explorer OL62 **Access** very limited
bus service from Alford to Bridge of
Buchat on the main road

Explore the atmospheric ruins of
Glenbuchat Castle before striding out
along a high ridge to take in wide views
and a peaceful landscape right on the
edge of the Cairngorms National Park.
Hillwalking gear and navigational skills
are advised.

The walk begins at Glenbuchat Castle,
just off the A97 between Strathdon and
Glenkindie. It was built in 1590 by John
Gordon of Cairnbarrow to celebrate his
marriage to wife Helen. The building is a
typical example of a z-plan towerhouse,
with a main large square room and two
rooms on either side forming a z shape as

seen from above. The ruin is roofless but
contains some impressive fireplaces and
carved stonework on the first floor.

To begin the walk, head back down the
access track from the castle car park to the
main road and turn left, crossing the
Bridge of Buchat, and then immediately
left again onto the minor road leading up
Glenbuchat. Continue up this quiet road
for just over 1km, passing Easter Buchat
farmhouse, before turning right along a
track to Blackhillock Farm. Keep right of
the larger sheds, with only a small stone
stone shed on your right. Pass through
two gates and follow the grassy track
uphill beyond, bearing slightly right at a
fork to stay on the main track. The next
gate is a deer gate in a high fence. Turn
right here and follow the fence to reach a
stile beyond the fence corner. Cross the
stile and accompany the fence uphill on a
faint path. Eventually, you meet a track;

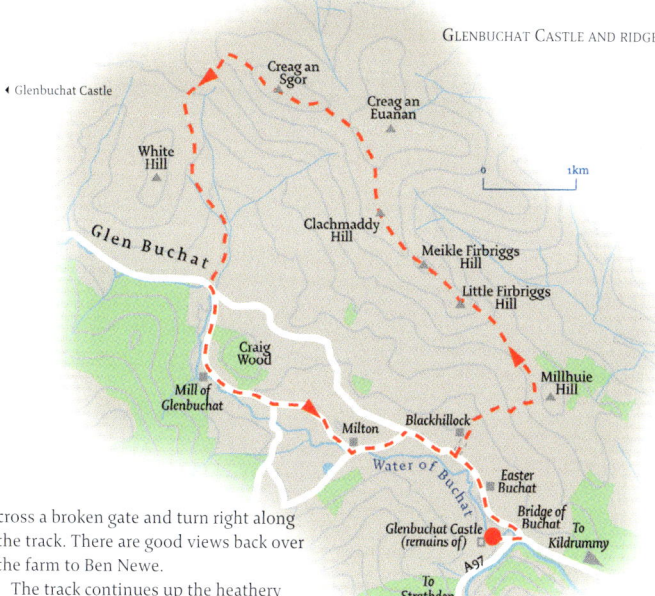

◄ Glenbuchat Castle

cross a broken gate and turn right along the track. There are good views back over the farm to Ben Newe.

The track continues up the heathery slopes of Millhuie Hill, and then swings left and descends slightly to the bealach. Pass through a gate and follow the track as it heads uphill once more, keeping left of a fence and soon reaching the top of Little Firbriggs Hill via a zigzag. The track then descends again to a second bealach. As the track ascends Clachmaddy Hill ignore a branch off left.

Follow the main track which cuts across the flank of Creag an Eunan towards the tor seen on Creag an Sgòr. The main track forks, bypassing the top of Creag an Sgòr to the right, but it's worth taking the fainter track over the top. The tor looks much more impressive from the far side. Descending from Creag an Sgòr, the main track is reached again – turn left along it.

Keep left at each of two forks to descend into Glen Buchat, and go left again at a third fork. Pass through a gate to reach a farm track and keep ahead along this to reach the road.

Turn left to begin the walk back to the castle, keeping right at a junction to follow the road past the Mill of Glenbuchat. At the next junction go left, and keep left again about 800m further on at Milton. When you reach a T-junction, turn right. The road now continues down the glen, joining the outward route. Follow it back to the junction with the A97 at the Bridge of Buchat, then turn right and right again to return to the start.

Ben Newe

Distance 3.75km **Time** 2 hours
Terrain forest tracks, paths, moorland,
steep in places **Map** OS Explorer 420
Access no public transport; nearest very
limited bus service from Alford to
Bellabeg, 2km from the start

This walk climbs up through forestry
before emerging onto open heather
topped with the rocky summit of Ben
Newe, a fantastic viewpoint.

The car park for this route is off the
minor road that starts 2km east of
Bellabeg in Strath Don and cuts over the
hills to Glen Buchat. Just past the house
at Altdachie, take the signed track which
branches right to reach the parking area

where there is an information board. Start
the walk by heading along the forest track
that continues in the same direction
(northwards) – there's a blue waymarker.
It passes above a forest pool popular
with dragonflies on balmy summer days
before beginning to climb steadily
through the trees.

By the edge of the forest, a marker post
indicates where to turn sharply right, still
following the main track uphill. Keep
straight ahead to another track junction
after 500m, then turn left following the
waymarker. After 250m, another marker
indicates where to turn right up a grassier
track. Ignore a track off right blocked by
fallen trees and continue to a fork. This

time bear right. After another 150m, you leave the forest tracks behind at last – turn left onto a path that climbs across heathery ground. There are multiple variants – keep following the occasional posts and heading uphill until you reach the summit of Ben Newe. You'll find a large rock outcrop – the depression cut into it is said to be a medieval holy well – and a trig point here, as well as a wooden seat. The views in all directions are superb.

Glen Buchat looks beautiful to the north, backed by the rolling hills and the outcrop on the summit of The Buck. Further right can be seen the ruins of Glenbuchat Castle and the winding River Don with the summits of Bennachie in the distance.For the descent, it's best to retrace your steps back the same way.

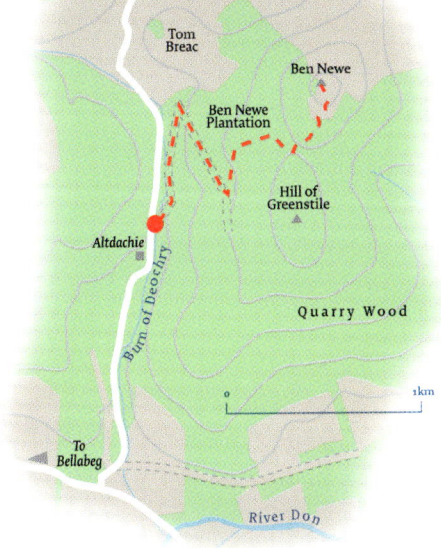

Bunzeach Trail from Bellabeg

Distance 6.75km **Time** 1 hour 30
Terrain forest tracks, paths, steep in
places **Map** OS Explorer OL59
Access very limited bus service from
Alford to Bellabeg

**The ancient motte castle of Invernochty
is by the start of this walk which leads
you through Bunzeach Forest for varied
views over picturesque Strath Don.**

Start from the car park at the west side
of the village of Bellabeg, where there is
also a picnic area. The Doune of
Invernochty dominates this end of the
village; the large mound is an earthwork
castle known as a motte which would
have been surrounded by a moat and is
thought to date back to 800AD. The
mound is large and steep and can be
climbed by taking the path on the far side
of the road. The castle stood at the
confluence of the Water of Nochty and the

River Bardock, and water was driven
through a complicated system of sluices
and dams to feed the moat.

Start the walk by heading past the
public toilets and following the River Don
to a minor road. Turn right along the road
to cross the bridge over the river. Soon it
leads to the attractive Strathdon Church,
its size testament to the once much larger
local population. Beyond the church, turn
left onto a smaller road and soon fork to
the right onto a track. Once past a turning
area, follow the forestry edge where there
are lovely views over Strath Don. The
track heads into the trees; at a crossroads
turn right and follow the track uphill,
which is overgrown in places, until it
reaches the crest of a rise.

When you reach a T-junction with a
clearer track, turn right, then right again
onto a narrow waymarked path amongst
dense conifers. Continuing through the

◀ Strath Don

forest, look out for a blue marker post which indicates the route turns left before descending steeply. It then bears right to follow a fence just above a minor road. Eventually, it bears right again, winding uphill through the trees. Part way up the slope, the route turns left through dense spruce plantations. On the far side of this, the path heads through a pedestrian gate and can become a little overgrown. There's another pedestrian gate leading out onto a junction with a narrow track. The circular walk continues with a right turn down this, but before going this way it is worth going left for a while to reach a viewpoint with a seat overlooking the church and Upper Strathdon. Return to the junction and follow the grassy track which leads down to the turning area from earlier in the walk. From here, head back to the road and church, and the start of the route.

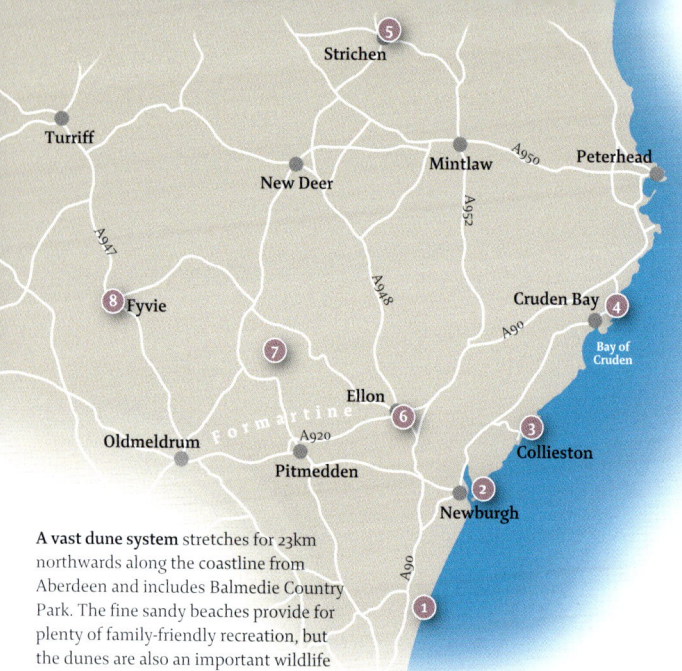

Map locations: Turriff, Strichen (5), New Deer, Mintlaw, Peterhead, Fyvie (8), Cruden Bay (4), Bay of Cruden, Ellon (6), Oldmeldrum, Pitmedden, Colliesson (3), Newburgh (2), (7), (1)

A947, A950, A952, A90, A948, Formartine, A920, A90

A vast dune system stretches for 23km northwards along the coastline from Aberdeen and includes Balmedie Country Park. The fine sandy beaches provide for plenty of family-friendly recreation, but the dunes are also an important wildlife habitat. The rare grasses support a wide variety of insects, birds and other wildlife. A number of watercourses snake their way through the dunes providing diverse wetlands. The Ythan Estuary, in particular, is prized by birdwatchers as a great place for spotting waders, as well as no less than four breeding varieties of tern.

Beyond the National Nature Reserve at Forvie, the coast takes on a rockier countenance, and the natural arches at the Bullers of Buchan are testament to the power of the waves. Visit in the spring to view the seabirds which come here to breed, creating a sky of white feathers above the foaming water below. Nearby

Slains Castle is said to have provided the inspiration for *Dracula* – it remains an eerie ruin perched on the high clifftop.

Inland, the countryside has a soft, rolling aspect dominated by large country estates and traditional agriculture. A short walk around Ellon passes near Ellon Castle Gardens, while the Georgian pile of Haddo House, which remained in the local Gordon family for more than 400 years, forms the focal point for another short stroll. Like Haddo, the enormous Fyvie Castle is managed by the National Trust for Scotland; both have beautiful grounds ideal for family walks.

Clifftop view to Slains Castle ▶

Formartine and the coast

Balmedie dunes and surf

Distance 2.25km **Time** 1 hour
Terrain dunes, beach, boardwalk path
and minor road **Map** OS Explorer 421
Access buses from Aberdeen to Balmedie,
500m from the start

The dunes and sands at Balmedie are a
great place to let the breeze blow the
cobwebs away and taste the salt spray
from the North Sea waves. Energetic
children will especially enjoy exploring
the Second World War fortifications and
the good play area.

Head for the north car park at Balmedie
Country Park, passing Balmedie House
to reach the Sand Bothy visitor centre
and children's play park. It matters little
which route is taken, with paths snaking
through the dunes to reach the sandy
beach beyond. This route heads directly
to the beach and then follows it south for
a while before heading back over the
dunes, passing the pillboxes to reach
the south car park and the road linking
the two car parks.

Start by heading right past the Sand
Bothy and play area to follow a tarmac
track which leads to a boardwalk. This
takes you through the dunes and out onto
the often windswept but beautifully
sandy beach.

Balmedie is part of an extensive dune
system which stretches for 23km all the
way from Aberdeen to the mouth of the
River Ythan at Newburgh. The shifting
dunes support marram and other grasses
which in turn provide a rich habitat for
wildlife – leading to the whole area being
designated a Site of Special Scientific
Interest. This protection did not prevent
Donald Trump getting planning
permission for a large-scale golf resort
and housing complex on the nearby
Menie Estate.

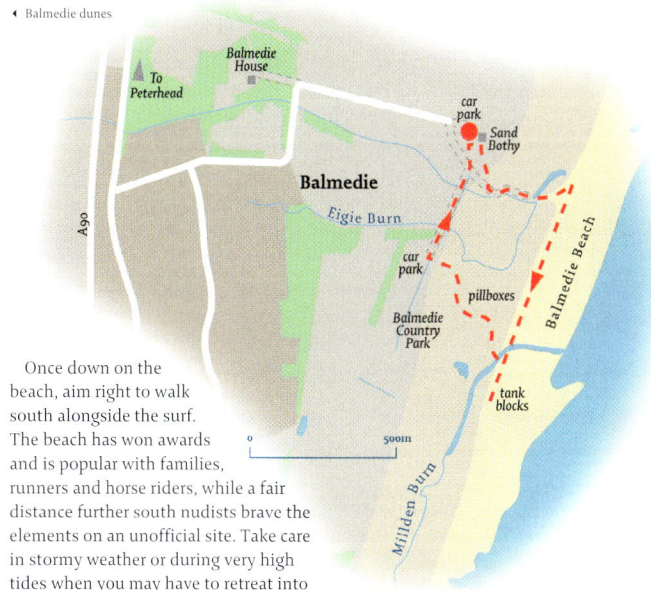

◄ Balmedie dunes

    Once down on the beach, aim right to walk south alongside the surf. The beach has won awards and is popular with families, runners and horse riders, while a fair distance further south nudists brave the elements on an unofficial site. Take care in stormy weather or during very high tides when you may have to retreat into the dunes; otherwise continue until you come to a river outflow, a good place for a spot of birdwatching.

    The way back over the dunes is found by retracing your steps about 50m along the beach to the last of the concrete anti-tank blocks. Here, you'll find a clear path up through the dunes to soon reach a boardwalk. Follow this as it weaves through the dunes, passing pillboxes built during the Second World War as part of the defences against an invasion from mainland Europe. These defensive lines exist all along this part of the coast and serve as an eerie reminder of the vulnerability of an island nation with so much remote coast to protect. Keep right when another boardwalk path joins from the left, then pass a picnic area with two more pillboxes high in the dunes to the right, before you reach the smaller south car park. From here, follow the surfaced road to the right to return to the start.

Ythan Estuary and Forvie Sands

Distance 5.75km **Time** 2 hours
Terrain path with dunes and sandy beach
Map OS Explorer 421 **Access** buses from
Aberdeen and Peterhead to Newburgh,
a short walk from the start

Bring your binoculars on this easy-going circuit to take in the superb birdlife of the estuary. The route crosses the dunes and beaches of the Forvie National Nature Reserve and passes the remains of a village which was buried by the constantly shifting sands. Dogs should be kept on a lead.

The coastline north of Aberdeen is characterised by long stretches of dunes, many of which have yet to fall prey to the demands of golf course developers. What might appear to be a fairly barren area of sand and grasses proves to be a much richer nature habitat on closer inspection. The meeting of these dunes with the tidal estuary of the River Ythan mean that this walk is bursting with biodiversity – four types of tern nest here, as well as one of the UK mainland's largest colonies of eider duck.

Begin the walk from the signed parking area on the east side of the A975 just north of the bridge over the River Ythan. Follow the blue waymarker along the track leading south through the trees, keeping straight ahead to skirt along the fringe of the tidal estuary. The mudflats here attract many waders, as well as rarities including shelduck, greater scaup, red-breasted merganser and velvet scoter. In summer, the resident population of eider ducks swells as they arrive to nest in the heather and long grass, filling the air with their distinctive 'owl-like' woo-ing calls.

Newburgh can be seen across the water; the distinctive building with the curved roof is part of the University of Aberdeen and specialises in underwater exploration using unmanned robots. As the path

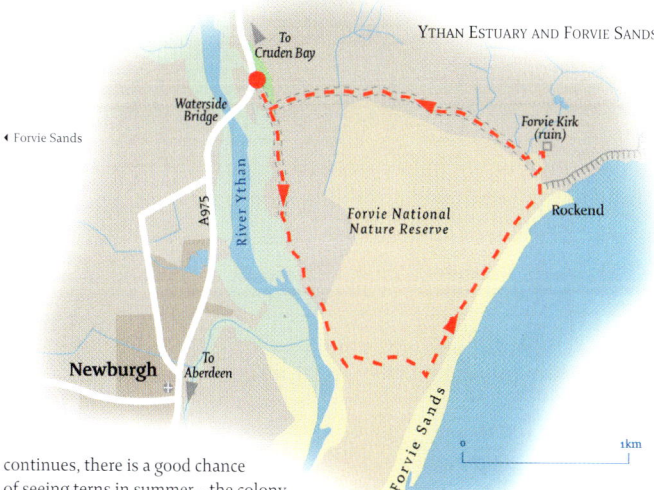

◄ Forvie Sands

continues, there is a good chance of seeing terns in summer – the colony here includes Arctic, little, common, and sandwich terns. Take care to keep to the path to avoid disturbing the nest sites. Once through a gate in a fence by a bench, look out for a marker post indicating where the route bears left up through a dip in the dunes before heading inland.

The path is well waymarked as it makes its way through the dune systems which form the bulk of the Forvie Sands National Nature Reserve. Eventually, the long sandy beach is reached; head left along the beach for around 1km. Just past a small burn a tall marker post indicates where to cut back inland, near the ruins of a salmon netting station which was still in use up until the 1980s.

At a junction adjacent to an information post (no 7), it is possible to shortcut the walk by simply continuing straight ahead. However, it is well worth turning right for a detour around the Forvie Village Trail.

This visits a series of information boards which tell the story of the settlement of Forvie before it was buried by the changing sands in the 1400s. Local lore tells of three sisters who were forced out to sea in a leaky boat in an attempt to deny them their inheritance. However, the sisters did reach land and laid a curse on the village by yelling, 'Let nocht bee funde in Furvye's glebes/Bot thystl, bente and sande', whereupon a storm raged bitterly for nine days until the village was completely buried by the sand.

The trail soon reaches one of the few remaining visible ruins, that of the old kirk. Turn left here and cross a footbridge to rejoin the main route where you turn right. At a junction, bear left, following the green waymarker to meet the outward path by the trees. Turn right to return to the start.

Collieston to Old Slains Castle

Distance 4.5km **Time** 2 hours
Terrain rough coastal path, track and
minor road **Map** OS Explorer 421
Access buses from Aberdeen and Ellon,
and limited buses from Fyvie to Collieston

This enjoyable circuit explores the
rough and wild coastal scenery north of
Collieston. Atop low cliffs, the ruins of
Old Slains Castle command a fantastic
position above the waves. The castle
shares its name with its newer cousin
near Cruden Bay.

On the north side of Collieston village is
a car park and viewpoint at St Catharine's
Dub, down by the sea. It is signed from
the road and has a superb outlook back
towards the village and over the harbour.
Traditionally, white fish were split open
and laid out to dry here in the sun to
produce the local delicacy, speldings.
These were eaten by T E Lawrence, better
known as Lawrence of Arabia, when he
stayed in a waterfront cottage here in 1930
while on leave from the RAF. He described
the dried fish as 'not bad', tasting like 'dull
veal', whilst also recording that the locals
were very keen on them and 'taste more in
them than I do'.

On foot, the car park can be reached
from the village by a short path above the
shore. At first glance, it appears the route
north from the car park is blocked by
cliffs. However, near the far end of the car
park is the start of a rocky staircase. After
a couple of steps it becomes a more
obvious path and climbs to the clifftop via
wooden steps. The headland below

St Catharine's Dub was the site of the shipwrecking of the *Santa Caterina*, a ship said to be carrying weapons for the Earl of Erroll as part of a planned plot against King James VI in 1594.

At the top of the steps, bear right to follow a narrow grassy path – this can be muddy in places – and head north along the coastline. Waves crashing on the rocky shore below provide a background rhythm to the walk, and soon the ruins of the Earl of Erroll's castle – Old Slains – can be seen ahead, with modern houses on either side.

Given the assault it suffered from cannons and gunpowder, it is surprising that so much remains today. The castle was originally built in the 13th century by the Comyn Earls of Buchan, the family that ruled medieval Buchan. During the Wars of Scottish Independence, it was forfeited by the family and gifted to Sir Gilbert Hay by Robert the Bruce in recognition of his support. The Hay family hung on to the castle until 1594, when Francis Hay, the 9th Earl of Erroll, led an unsuccessful rebellion against James VI. It was during the aftermath that the castle was violently destroyed and Hay exiled. On return from exile, he built New Slains Castle on the site of an older building further up the coast near Cruden Bay.

Before you come to the ruins, a rocky islet just offshore is passed and then the path crosses a stile and curves left around the back of a bay, the sea stack of Hummel Craig visible below. Nearer to the castle, the path almost peters out. Stay near the fence and then descend to reach an access track. Below can be seen the sandy beach of Broad Haven.

From the castle, follow the track inland, passing a farm and cottage before emerging on a minor road. Turn left along this to head back to Collieston. At Kirkton of Slains, turn left at two junctions to return to the viewpoint car park at the start.

◄ Old Slains Castle

The Bullers of Buchan

Distance 4.5km **Time** 1 hour 45 (one way)
Terrain rough coastal path, steep cliffs
Map OS Explorer 427 **Access** buses from
Aberdeen and Peterhead to Cruden Bay;
bus stop at the Bullers of Buchan

This dramatic coastal walk passes the
eerie clifftop ruins of Slains Castle, the
inspiration for *Dracula*, on the way to the
Bullers of Buchan. This natural wonder
is where a collapsed sea cave has produced
a massive blowhole and numerous arches
and caves. A bus can be caught back to
Cruden Bay, or you could walk back by the
same route.

Cruden Bay is an attractive village
renowned for its golf course and proximity
to Slains Castle. If driving, leave the A975

opposite the hotel and follow Main Street
past the post office to reach a parking area
on the left. Start by taking the path
through the trees that leaves from the far
end of the car park. Keep left at the fork to
cross the river and then stay right and
follow the river downstream through a red
sandstone gully. The path climbs gently to
the left, past the remains of a brick doocot,
to follow the coastline.

Soon, the massive outline of Slains
Castle comes into view. Bram Stoker
stayed in the area for a number of
summers and the castle is said to have
inspired his most famous creation, Count
Dracula. The first castle was built here at
the end of the 16th century to replace Old
Slains Castle near Collieston. It remained

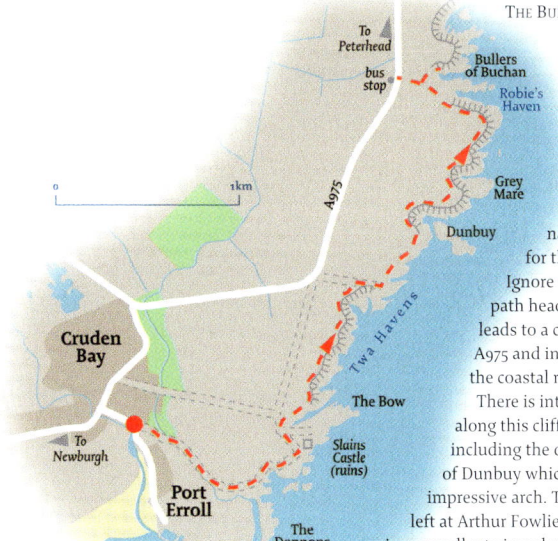

natural moat for the castle. Ignore the straight path heading left which leads to a car park on the A975 and instead keep on the coastal route.

There is interest all along this clifftop section, including the detached rock of Dunbuy which sports an impressive arch. The path curves left at Arthur Fowlie, where there is an excellent view along the coast towards Boddam. The rocky drama continues on the next section where the path is rough and close to the cliff edge in places until the cottages at the Bullers of Buchan are reached. A track here leads up to the bus stop and car park on the main road.

Before heading up to the road for the bus (or retracing your steps to Cruden Bay), continue past the cottages to view the blowhole that gives the place its name. The outer wall of the massive collapsed sea cave is breached by two natural arches. Extreme care should be taken on the narrow path – do not be tempted onto the slippery grass which tops the sheer cliffs. The Bullers are popular with nesting seabirds, including puffins, guillemots, shags and kittiwakes.

in the hands of the Earls of Erroll, a powerful local family, for more than 300 years, and was enlarged and remodelled many times. After a period of disrepair and restoration following a change of ownership, the roof was taken off in 1925 to avoid taxes and the castle has been crumbling away ever since.

Rejoining the coast path on the far side of the castle is somewhat awkward. Head inland beside the fence and follow the track for a short distance. Watch out for stone steps sticking out of the wall on the right and a marker post on the far side. Climb the wall here and follow a faint path running on the inland side of a deep seawater inlet which provides a

◀ Natural arch, the Bullers of Buchan

Mormond White Horse

Distance 7.75km **Time** 3 hours
Terrain minor road, track, paths,
pathless moorland **Map** OS Explorer 427
Access no public transport to the start

**The highest hill in the northeastern
corner is usually referred to as Mormond
Hill, whilst its highest point, visited here,
is called Waughton Hill. The flanks of the
hill include a White Horse, visited on this
walk, and a stag, better seen from the
countryside to the south.**

Start from the High Street in Strichen
which has plenty of on-street parking, as
well as a couple of shops and the
imposing castellated town house. Begin
the walk by heading northwest along the
High Street, away from the town house
towards a prominent church. Turn right
here to follow West Street which then
becomes Hospital Brae as it climbs uphill.
As it leaves the village, the road narrows

and swings right, and later bears sharp
left providing a first view of the White
Horse on the flanks of the hill. Usually
known as the Mormond White Horse, it
was constructed in the 1790s by Captain
Fraser, the local laird, on his return from
the Napoleonic War. It is said that during
the ultimately ill-fated Flanders
campaign, the Captain's horse was shot
from under him in battle and his sergeant
offered his own mount as a replacement.
As they were changing horses, Sergeant
Hutcheon was shot and killed and the
White Horse serves as a memorial to him.

Follow the lane to Bransburn, and turn
right at a crossroads beyond by a small
wind turbine. The lane becomes a muddy
track after the farm as you head directly
towards the hill; keep straight on as the
going becomes grassy underfoot. When
the grassy track ends at a gate, turn left
through another gate to cross a field,

◄ View from the White Horse

following the
waymarker. Go
through the kissing
gate and turn right
up a path that winds
steeply in places,
through gorse
bushes, to emerge
at the White Horse.

Measuring over
5om in length, the
horse is constructed
from local quartz and is
maintained by volunteers.
As well as fabulous views over
the Aberdeenshire countryside, the
horse is said to grant the wish of anyone
who completes three turns whilst
standing on the horse's eye.

From the horse, continue uphill until
you reach a grassy track, where you turn
right. After 100m, turn left onto another
grassy track to climb towards a large stone
ruin. Known as the Hunter's Lodge, it was
built by the same Captain Fraser who
constructed the horse and was said to
have had a fireplace large enough to roast
a deer. The door lintel bears the words; 'In
this Hunter's Lodge Rob Gibb commands
MDCCLXXIX'. The name Rob Gibb is said
to have been used as a secret code by
Jacobites toasting their support of Bonnie
Prince Charlie.

From the lodge the route now crosses
pathless terrain to reach the summit of
Waughton Hill. Take a faint path from the

left corner of Hunter's Lodge to head
slightly downhill, aiming northwest into
a dip before climbing again, following a
line of old posts. The high point at 234m
is marked with a couple of wooden posts
and a tiny cairn amidst the tussocky grass.
Nearby Mormond Hill (230m) can be seen
with masts on the top just to the east.

Head back to the dip and then aim
southwest to reach the right side of a line
of trees. Turn right onto a track, keeping
left at a fork to descend to an old quarry.
Keep to the right of this to reach a track
leading to a junction; turn left to head
downhill. Go through a gate, keeping to
the right of a larger quarry, and after 150m
turn left to rejoin the outward route near
the wind turbine. Keep straight on here to
return to Bransburn and then Strichen.

69

Ellon and Ythan riverside

Distance 4km **Time** 1 hour 30
Terrain waymarked route on paths and
pavements **Map** OS Explorer 421
Access regular buses from Aberdeen,
Oldmeldrum and Inverurie to Ellon

**This short exploration of Ellon, 'the
Gateway to Buchan', takes in the woods
and riverside as well as the stone
buildings of this small town.**

The best place to start is the riverside
car park (parking charge) just off Market
Street, a short stroll from the town centre.
Start downstream by the River Ythan,
heading left as you face the river. The
Ythan supports a diverse range of wildlife,
from herons and swans to salmon, trout
and otters. In past centuries, it was famed
as a source of pearls from freshwater
mussels. Now a highly protected species,
one pearl found here was of such quality
that it was presented to King James VI and

become one of the brightest jewels in the
Scottish crown.

Follow the surfaced walkway and
immediately after the houses turn left to
follow a rough path up to Castle Road
with a wall on your left. Cross the main
road and turn left along the pavement
beside a high stone wall. The is part of
the Deer Dyke, built in the mid-19th
century as a make-work scheme to
alleviate unemployment as well as to
enclose the formal deer park attached to
Ellon Castle. At the war memorial, turn
right up Schoolhill Road, although you
might want to detour alongside the
estate agent's office to see the impressive
ancient coat of arms of the Kennedy
family – including boars' heads and
crossed keys. This once adorned the
tolbooth building which was demolished
in the 1840s.

Follow Schoolhill Road past the access

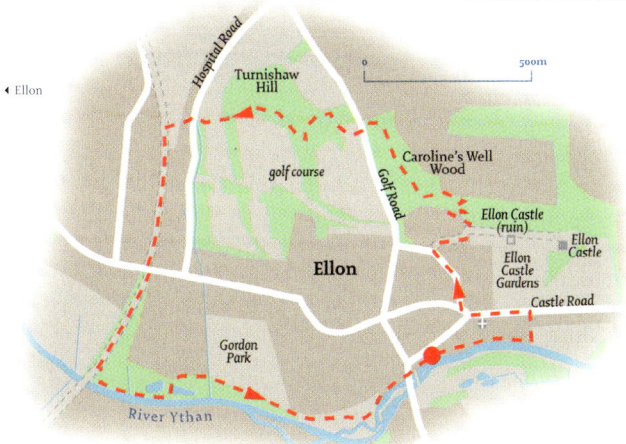

road to the health centre on your right and take the next right (still Schoolhill Road) towards the car park for Ellon Castle Gardens. Open to the public, the walled garden features beautiful floral displays and fruit trees. Unless detouring to the gardens, bear left up the ramped walkway next to the steps to enjoy views back down over Ellon and the ruins of the old castle by the walled garden.

Follow the surfaced path to the left and just before it emerges into the housing turn left onto a rough path and head downhill through the trees. This is Caroline's Well Wood, named after Caroline Hamilton Gordon who lived at Ellon Castle at the beginning of the 20th century. Just before the bottom of the dip turn right and continue through the wood to reach Golf Road at a small gateway. Cross over and follow the path opposite for a short distance before bearing right.

Although the trees here have suffered storm damage in recent years, it remains a good place to spot red squirrels.

Follow the path as it curves uphill, ignoring two paths on the left and turning right at a third junction. At a bench overlooking the golf course take the rough path ahead, soon going down steps and reaching Hospital Road. Cross over and dogleg left and then right onto a path leading to the Formartine & Buchan Way. Turn left along it and when it reaches a road, cross and rejoin the cyclepath, following the sign for Udny Station.

A high stone viaduct is soon seen ahead, rebuilt in 1861 after the original collapsed within a year. Rather than cross over, take the path to the left down to the riverside path and follow it past Ellon's pump track and cycle track. Continue along the riverside to go under the new and old bridges before returning to the start.

Haddo House circuit

Distance 4.25km **Time** 1 hour 30
Terrain level waymarked paths,
sometimes muddy **Map** OS Explorer 426
Access no public transport to the start

**The parkland around Haddo House
boasts specimen trees, swathes of
rhododendrons, a man-made loch with
bird hides and a children's play area. The
grand stately home and gardens are also
worth a visit and, together with the
courtyard café, add up to a full day out.**

Haddo House is well signed north of
Tarves from the B999 and south of
Methlick from the B9005. The house and
country park share the car park (charge)
and there is an information board
detailing the waymarked routes here. This
walk combines the red and blue routes.

The Haddo Estate is steeped in
agriculture, including the name which
derives from the word *davoch* – used to
describe the amount of land which could
be ploughed by an ox in a day. 'Haddo'
comes from the phrase for half a davoch.
The estate lands remaining today are a
mixture of shooting estate and farmland,
with the house itself managed by the
National Trust for Scotland.

Start the walk by heading to the stable
block, turning right as you reach it and
keeping straight ahead on the main path.
At a fork by a huge beech tree, keep right
to reach the ornately decorated
pheasantry. Pheasant and wildfowl
shooting has always been important to
the estate as the grandeur of this building
shows. Today, much of the land
surrounding the park is used for rearing
pheasants. Walk along the back of the
building before soon branching right and
then keeping straight ahead as you pass
a children's play area. Turn right at a
T-junction to pass between two lakes,

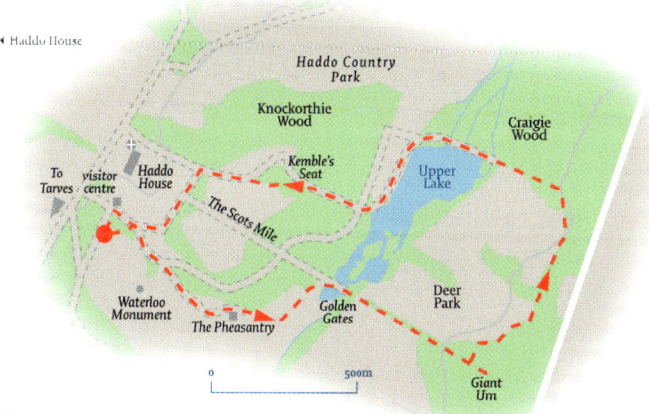

◀ Haddo House

Haddo Country Park

Knockorthie Wood

Craigie Wood

Kemble's Seat

To Tarves

visitor centre

Haddo House

Upper Lake

The Scots Mile

Deer Park

Waterloo Monument

Golden Gates

The Pheasantry

Giant Urn

0   500m

following the path to the ornate gates of the deer park. The Gordon family have lived on the estate for more than five centuries, building Haddo House in 1732, their previous residence having been burnt down by the Covenanters during the 'killing years'. The present-day parkland was set out by the Fourth Earl of Aberdeen, George Hamilton-Gordon, in the 1800s.

Go through the gates and head straight on up the slope, passing two fine deer sculptures before reaching the massive stone urn at the top of the hill. The urn and deer commemorate the Fourth Earl's wife, who died of tuberculosis, and his children. There are glorious views from here back down to Haddo House. Retrace your steps to the deer sculptures and then take the path off to the right to undulate along the edge of the woodland. Further on, ignore a gate and instead follow the path curving left downhill.

At the bottom, keep straight ahead to pass through a gap in a fence, cross a footbridge and keep straight ahead to cross the dam at the north end of the main lake, passing a covered shelter with fine views over the water.

Fork left at the far end of the dam onto a grassy path that follows the shoreline. After passing a bird hide, you come to a junction by a seat. Take the path curving right, then go straight ahead at the next junction. Soon after passing another children's play area, go left to emerge at the front of the house.

Haddo is a grand stately pile built in the Georgian Palladian style, complete with a chapel to one side. During the Second World War, it was commandeered as a maternity hospital and nearly 1200 local babies were born here. You could turn right here to visit the gardens (and house if open – charge payable) or carry on ahead to follow the track back to the start.

Fyvie Castle forest walk

Distance 4.5km **Time** 1 hour 30
Terrain minor road, waymarked estate
paths, woodland **Map** OS Explorer 426
Access buses from Aberdeen, Turriff and
Oldmeldrum to Fyvie

**Test your supernatural sleuthing powers
on this short walk to one of the most
haunted castles in Scotland. Even if the
ghosts don't reveal themselves, the
towers of Fyvie Castle are sure to impress
and the route takes in a loch teeming
with wildlife.**

Fyvie sits part way between Turriff and
Oldmeldrum on the A947 and is one of
many impressive castles and stately
homes in the area. This walk starts from
opposite the Co-op on the southwestern
side of the village (car park opposite),
reached by turning onto the B9005. Head
towards the castle grounds by walking

uphill past the war memorial and taking
the next road on the left. Part way along,
a gap in the hedge leads to a woodland
path; when this descends to a track with
the entrance gates to the castle on the left,
go straight ahead onto a forestry track.

Just before the loch, fork left, following
yellow arrows to cross the outflow and
pass a small dam. The path crosses the
castle driveway a couple of times before
following a lochside path and then
heading through a gate in the garden
wall. The loch and parkland surrounding
the castle were laid out in the 19th
century, but the castle itself dates from
the 13th century, though it has undergone
a number of radical extensions and
alterations since then. In fact, it is said
that the five families to own Fyvie –
Preston, Meldrum, Seton, Gordon and
Forbes-Leith – each added a tower to this

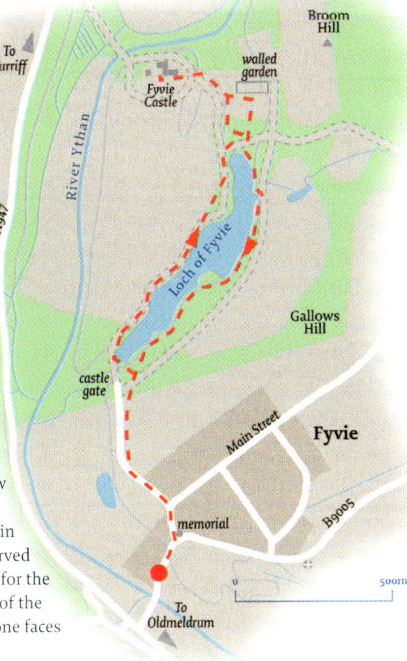

◄ Fyvie Castle

Scots baronial fortress. Certainly, the castle has seen its fair share of famous historical faces, with Robert the Bruce who held an open-air court here and Charles I who lived here as a child.

Keep left to enter the Rhymers Haugh Garden and then follow the path to the left side of the car park. The gardens and grounds are open all year, but the castle itself, which is owned by the National Trust for Scotland, is open between April and October. Go through the ornate gate and follow the driveway to head around the impressive building. From the main entrance, adorned with a huge carved coat of arms, go left and look out for the massive steel bands holding one of the towers upright and the carved stone faces peering down.

As well as an indelible blood stain, the castle is said to boast at least two ghosts, including one known as the green lady. During renovations in the 20th century, a skeleton was unearthed from one of the walls and re-buried at the same spot, after which the hauntings are said to have diminished. Visitors are, however, guaranteed sightings of the magnificent stone wheel staircase, extensive art collection and Edwardian interiors.

From the castle, return to the car park and, if you like, detour through the walled gardens dating back to the 18th century, and planted in more recent times with Scottish fruits and vegetables. From the far side of the car park, take the straight path through the avenue of trees and up stone steps to reach a gate. Now follow the yellow arrows around the far side of the loch, passing a boathouse and bird hide to eventually rejoin the outward route and return to Fyvie.

75

Garioch is at the heart of Aberdeenshire, the main settlement of Inverurie being set amidst fertile and productive farmland. The history of the town reaches back for more than a thousand years – but the Garioch has been inhabited for far longer. Few areas of Scotland are richer in archaeological remains, from the fine stone circle at Easter Aquhorthies to the Ogham inscriptions on the Pictish-carved Brandesbutt Stone. Those prepared to walk can experience this ancient heritage at the hillforts on Tap o' Noth, the Hill of Dunnideer and on Mither Tap.

The area is dominated by Bennachie, an isolated mass of moorland; its highest summit is Oxen Craig, but it is the nearby peak of Mither Tap whose distinctive profile has become such a familiar landmark.

North of Garioch is Strathbogie and its capital Huntly, close to the border with Moray. The fine grey stone buildings

around the square are impressive, but it is the magnificent castle ruins that draw many here. Though Huntly appears well-connected, with both the railway and several main roads converging here, all can change dramatically in the winter when the area often suffers from heavy snowfalls. The town is home to Britain's only all-weather crosscountry skiing facilities at the Nordic & Outdoor Centre.

Garioch and Huntly

Millstone Hill Trail

Distance 4.75km **Time** 2 hours
Terrain clear waymarked paths, rocky and
steep in places **Map** OS Explorer 421
Access no public transport to the start

Millstone Hill is one of the less known
of the hills which together make up
Bennachie. Sitting slightly aloof from
the other peaks, it makes a fabulous
viewpoint; this circuit climbs from dense
forest through pinewoods to reach the
open moorland above.

The walk starts from the Donview car
park on the south side of the Bennachie
massif, 2km north of Monymusk on the
minor road along the north side of the
River Don. There are toilets here, as well
as information about the waymarked
routes. This route follows the green
waymarked Millstone Hill Trail. The
whole Bennachie range is very popular
with walkers, cyclists, runners and
orienteers. Footpath upgrading work has
done much to combat erosion and regular
maintenance work is carried out by the
Bailies of Bennachie, a voluntary
conservation society who also run events
in and around the area.

From the back of the car park, take the
left-hand path heading uphill. It soon joins
a track where it bears right through a gate
and then straight ahead onto a path once
more, passing some magnificent mature
beech trees. Watch for the marker post
which indicates a right turn to continue
uphill and, a little later, a left turn. After
bearing to the right again, the path
becomes steeper with steps in places.

As the trees of the main woodland begin
to thin they are replaced by scattered pines

◀ View of Mither Tap
from Millstone Hill

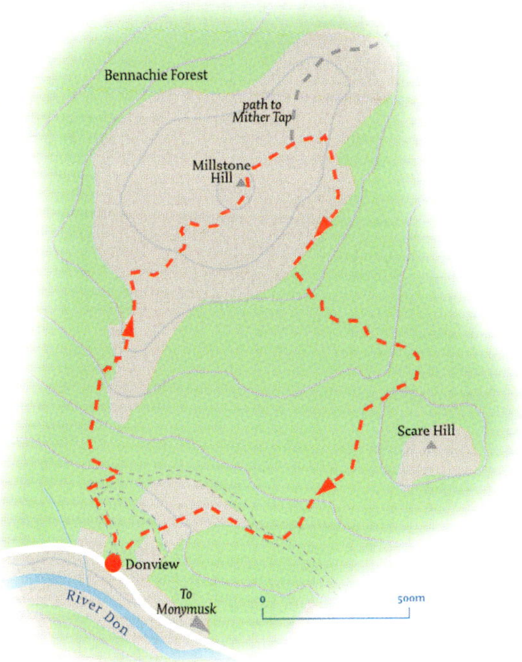

and birches, the pioneer tree which thrives in the more marginal conditions where other species struggle. A large slab of stone provides a good respite spot from the climb. Now the heather of the open moorland starts to dominate and, on a clear day, Lochnagar is visible in the far distance. The final climb to the summit of Millstone Hill is rewarded by a fantastic view of the rocky tor of Mither Tap straight ahead, as well as back over Donside.

Take the path heading northeast towards Mither Tap from the summit. At the path junction, keep straight on; the route soon bends to the right to traverse the side of the hill. Descending, it reaches the dense conifers of the plantations originally forested in the 1950s – before then the area was a mixture of moorland, open grazing land and cultivated crofts. Cross three forestry tracks, enjoying the fleeting views from the many breaks in the forest as the path returns to the parking area at Donview.

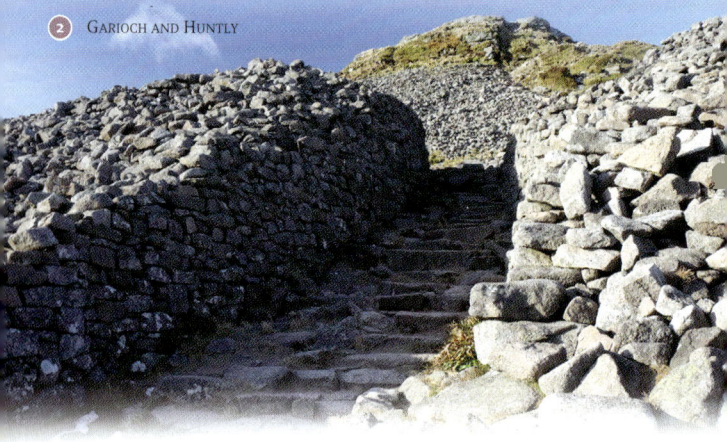

Mither Tap

Distance 6km **Time** 2 hours 30
Terrain well-graded waymarked paths,
rocky summit on exposed moorland
Map OS Explorer 421 **Access** no public
transport to the start

**Conquer the most dramatic of the
Bennachie summits to experience your
own 'king of the castle' moment atop its
rocky granite tor, surrounded by the ruins
of an ancient hillfort.**

Start from the Bennachie Visitor Centre
(parking charge), which is well signed to
the south of Chapel of Garioch. This route
takes the main path, waymarked in green
as the Mither Tap Timeline Trail, before
descending via an alternative route,
joining part of the Gordon Way for the
return. Facing the information board,
head left to follow the wide path through
the trees alongside a burn.

Keep straight ahead at the next two
junctions, following the green markers.
When the Gordon Way heads left, bear
right instead to pass a bench and soon
reach the remains of a building.

Bennachie was once commonland
where local people could dig peats, quarry
stone and graze livestock. Pressure for
land caused it to be settled by squatters in
the early 19th century and a community
existed here for about 50 years. In 1859,
the local landowners succeeded in a court
action which divided the 'commonty'
between themselves; they then began
charging rents. Most residents of the
community on Bennachie were forced to
leave as they could not afford to pay; the
settlement eventually died out, leaving
only the ruins seen today.

The route soon delves amongst the
pines; keep on the waymarked trail which
aims right and continues uphill. At a
T-junction, turn right and then left into

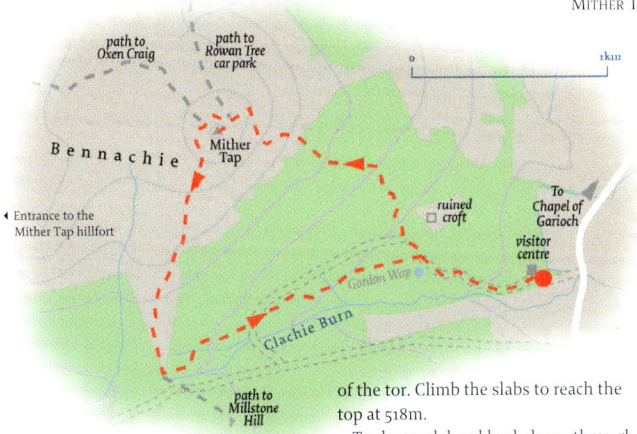

path to Oxen Craig
path to Rowan Tree car park
Bennachie
Mither Tap
Entrance to the Mither Tap hillfort
ruined croft
To Chapel of Garioch
visitor centre
Gordon Way
Clachie Burn
path to Millstone Hill
1km

trees. As you gain height, the natural treeline is reached and the pitched stone path begins the climb through heather to Mither Tap. Bennachie boasts nine distinct summits – Mither Tap is by far the most prominent with its distinctive outline and position overlooking the coastal plains, though Oxen Craig is actually higher at 528m. The patchwork landscape of rural Aberdeenshire opens out below as the path gains height and Millstone Hill comes into view on the left.

Nearing the top, ignore the path to the Rowan Tree car park and instead continue ahead towards the two walls of the ancient hillfort. The stones would have been carried up from the lower slopes to build these walls in prehistoric and Pictish times. The path leads through the fort's main entrance, with the remains of the old parapet walk visible on one of the walls. The fortress guards the only side of the summit not protected by the granite cliffs

of the tor. Climb the slabs to reach the top at 518m.

To descend, head back down through the main entrance of the fort, turning left at a junction onto a clear path which curves around the back of Mither Tap. Stay on the main path as it bears left and keep a sharp eye out for a junction – turn left here to follow a pitched path which runs fairly steeply downhill.

The peak ahead is Millstone Hill and this path leads directly to it if you have energy to spare. After passing through birch and rowan trees and then pines, you come to a junction of three paths. To begin the walk back, turn left here onto the Gordon Way, part of an 18.5km walk along old peat-extraction paths linking Bennachie with Suie. This section heads through plantations, swinging sharp left at one point before emerging onto a wide track. Cross this, aiming slightly left, to remain on the Gordon Way. Eventually, you reach a junction with the outward route; turn right to return to the car park and the Bennachie Visitor Centre.

Oxen Craig and the tops of Bennachie

Distance 9.25km **Time** 3 hours 30
Terrain good paths, exposed high ground,
rocky in places **Map** OS Explorer OL62
Access buses from Inverurie and Huntly
stop at Oyne, a short walk from the start

**This moorland hike takes in the two
highest peaks of Bennachie whilst enjoying
sweeping views; it also visits the less
known tor of Craigshannoch before
returning through woodland.**

The Back o'Bennachie car park is located
just off the B9002 west of the village of
Oyne; it is signed from the road. There is an
information board here, as well as toilets
and a picnic area. This route follows the
brown waymarked Quarry Trail past the
information board to climb gently through
the trees to a track. Dogleg to the right and
then left to continue on a path which soon
crosses a burn by a wooden seat. Ignore the

path to the right and another to the left just
after an artwork.

As the path climbs, it leaves the trees
behind to enter steeper heather-clad
terrain. A signed path to the right provides
a short detour to visit Little Oxen Craig; if
taking this, you must return to continue to
the main summit. As the top comes into
view, bear right at a fork for the final climb
to the rocky tor of Oxen Craig. This peak is
slightly higher than Mither Tap, topping
out at 528m, although there is only 10m in
this sibling peak rivalry. A view indicator
helps to make sense of the extensive
panorama. Retrace your steps briefly before
heading down a flight of stone steps on
the right to begin the traverse to the
prominent peak of the Mither Tap.

Keep straight ahead at the path junction,
turning right at the next one. The other
path leads to Craigshannoch which is

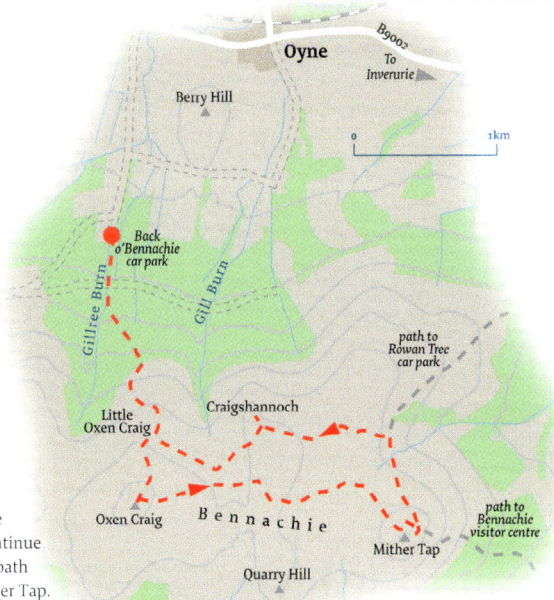

visited on the return, so continue on the main path towards Mither Tap. At the foot of the tor, ignore a path to the right; instead climb steeply left to pass the crags before bearing right through the deep walls of piled stones, the remains of an Iron Age fort which guards the summit. The view from the granite crown shows why the Mither Tap is so prominent in distant views, as much of Aberdeenshire is seen as on a map. You can also look down on other walkers directly below and appreciate the defensive qualities of the 4000-year-old fort.

For the return, go back through the main entrance to the fort and take the path leading straight ahead, known as the Maiden Causeway. It is likely that this was the route employed to transport the stones for the double walls of the fort. After heading gently downhill, take a left turn at the next junction to climb towards Craigshannoch. A short detour to the right reaches a cairn with a fine view. At a T-junction bear right, then right again to reach the summit. From here, return to the main path and follow it until it meets the outward route near Little Oxen Craig. Turn right here to retrace your steps into the forestry and down to the Back o'Bennachie car park.

◀ Towards Mither Tap on the Bennachie plateau

Hill of Dunnideer

Distance 5.25km **Time** 2 hours
Terrain steep grassy path, farmland paths
which can get muddy, short section on
road **Map** OS Explorer OL62 **Access** the
nearest bus stop is at Insch, 1.5km away

**The short climb up the Hill of Dunnideer is
well worth the effort. The summit is
crowned by the ruins of a medieval castle
built on the site of an ancient hillfort.
The relatively flat landscape surrounding
Insch ensures extensive 360-degree views.**

The Hill of Dunnideer lies just to the
west of Insch and there is a lay-by for
parking at the start of the walk. To reach it,
take Western Road in Insch and look
for the lay-by up a slope on the left,
marked by a plinth, after about 1km. An
information board gives some detail of the
Iron Age hillfort on the summit –
archaeologists believe at least two forts
were built on the site at different times.

Head through the kissing gate and turn
right to climb up alongside the fence.
As you gain height, the views over Insch
steadily improve. At the top of the field,
go through the gate and continue up the
now open hill, following the sign. The
mainly underground remains of the forts
are crossed in at least two bands on the
final stage of the ascent, but are hard to
perceive on the ground. Much of the
research here was undertaken through
digs and from aerial photographs.
Together, these revealed the Iron Age
structures that were composed partly of
vitrified stone – rocks which were fused
together through the creation of a vast
amount of heat.

As you reach the flat summit, the
remains of Dunnideer Castle are much
more obvious. It is thought that this may
be one of the earliest stone castles in
Scotland, possibly dating back to 1260. The

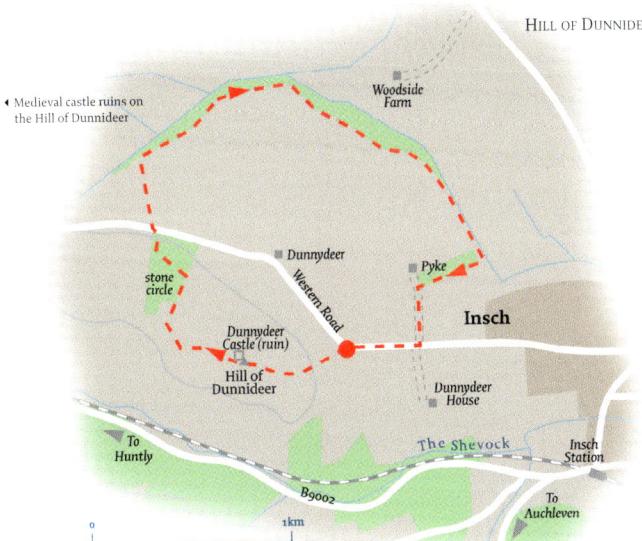

◄ Medieval castle ruins on the Hill of Dunnideer

existing fort was raided for stones to build the simple tower which would probably have had two floors. The sturdiness of the castle is still in evidence – the walls would have been 1.9m thick when first built.

Equally impressive are the far-reaching views. The twin peak of the Hill of Christ's Kirk lies just to the south and the tor-topped summits of Bennachie are easily recognised to its left. Tap o' Noth, which is the site of a much larger hillfort, is prominent against the skyline to the west and the agricultural heartland of rural Aberdeenshire surrounds Insch itself.

Carry on past the castle and head downhill, bearing left at a waymarker through a path in the gorse. Follow the path between fences and after a gate turn right uphill to soon pass the three remaining stones of a Bronze Age stone circle. Continue ahead and at a junction about halfway down the slope bear left through the trees before curving right downhill to a kissing gate leading back to the minor road. Cross and go through the gate to pick up the path signposted for Insch, which runs around the edge of a field before turning right between fields and wildlife-rich native woodland.

Continue on this path, eventually passing through a pair of kissing gates. After a third kissing gate, keep straight ahead, ignoring a path into the trees on the right, cross a small burn and then take the path to the right, soon reaching a track. Turn left here to reach the road from Insch, then turn right to head uphill along the road back to the start.

Leith Hall

Distance 3km **Time** 1 hour
Terrain waymarked paths and tracks
Map OS Explorer OL62 **Access** buses from
Huntly and Inverurie to Leith Hall

**Explore the varied parkland and farmland
surrounding impressive Leith Hall, a castle
in all but name.**

Originally built as a towerhouse in
around 1650, Leith Hall has undergone a
number of elaborate extensions, resulting
in the elegant Scots baronial pile seen
today. Owned by the Leith-Hay family, the
house was a typical laird's residence
complete with French-style turrets,
courtyard and extensive gardens and
parkland. It was bequeathed to the
National Trust for Scotland in 1945 and the
gardens and parkland remain open all year
round. The hall itself is open for guided
tours several days a week from June to
September, with weekend tours only in
spring and autumn. There is also a café.

An information board in the car park
(charge) has a map of several waymarked
walks on the estate. This route combines
the pond walk with the Kirkhill circuit.
Turn right at the board as you face the hall
and follow a wide track, soon bearing left
alongside a burn. At an ornate bridge, turn
right and then, once over it, left to follow
the blue marker and reach the pond.
Created as part of the landscaping for
Leith Hall, it has an attractive boathouse
at the far end. You may catch a whiff of
the angel's share from the Ardmore
Distillery which can be seen across the
fields on the left.

Keep left at a junction and you'll shortly
reach a millstone overlooking the water.
Bear left again here and soon there is an
optional detour on the left which visits a

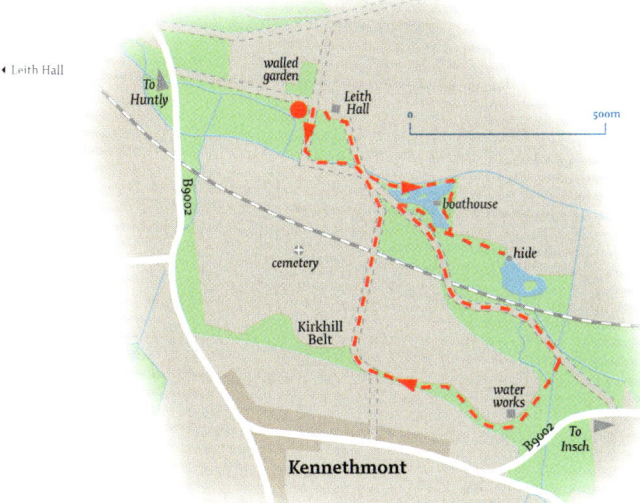

◄ Leith Hall

bird hide. The rough path meanders through the trees to reach the wooden hide overlooking another pond. In summer, the water is busy with breeding pairs of mallard and moorhen and if you are very lucky you might spot the resident otter. In the winter months, the pond is home to overwintering mute swans, wigeon, teal and goldeneye ducks. From the hide, return to the main path and keep following the blue markers to reach a straight track. Turn left here, soon passing the 19th-century ice house and now following green waymarkers in reverse.

The route soon crosses the railway line where there is a good view back to the Tap o' Noth in the distance. Follow the path through woodland – ignoring a turning – until just before a stone bridge.

Turn right before the bridge to follow a path, soon crossing over a smaller wooden bridge and alongside fields at the edge of the wood. Go straight across the waterworks access track and keep to the path as it bears right, following a fence. Just before a farm gateway, turn right on a path marked for Leith Hall which leads down to the railway line.

A short detour left here leads to the old churchyard, dating back to medieval times. Cross the railway bridge and turn left onto the wide path. Keep right at a fork to return to Leith Hall and bear left along the side of the building to reach the front, near the start of the walk.

Huntly Castle and the River Deveron

Distance 4km **Time** 1 hour
Terrain narrow riverside path, sometimes muddy, surfaced cycleways and pavement
Map OS Explorer 425 **Access** regular trains and buses from Aberdeen, Inverurie and Inverness to Huntly

Explore the attractive centre of Huntly and its surrounding countryside, passing the ancient castle before following the banks of the River Deveron.

Huntly is a friendly market town with lovely stone buildings. For centuries it was known as Milton of Strathbogie, but changed to Huntly when it was remodelled as a planned town in the 18th century by the Duke of Gordon. Long an important stopping place on the main turnpike road from Inverness to Aberdeen (now the A96), its importance increased with the coming of the railway in 1854.

Start from the Market Muir free car park around 600m south of the town square and walk up Gordon Street through the town square. Continue up Castle Street, passing the public toilets on the left, and keep straight on at the next junction to follow The Avenue past the war memorial.

The impressive gateway ahead belongs to the Gordon Schools. Go through it and follow the avenue of trees ahead, passing the playing fields, Cooper Park car park and a children's play area. The great bulk of Huntly Castle can be seen ahead with the visitor car park on the left beneath the trees.

Even a brief glance reveals the great splendour of the castle, famous for its fine heraldic sculptures, richly carved fireplaces and inscribed stone friezes. The castle was built as the seat of the Huntly Clan and remained so for five centuries.

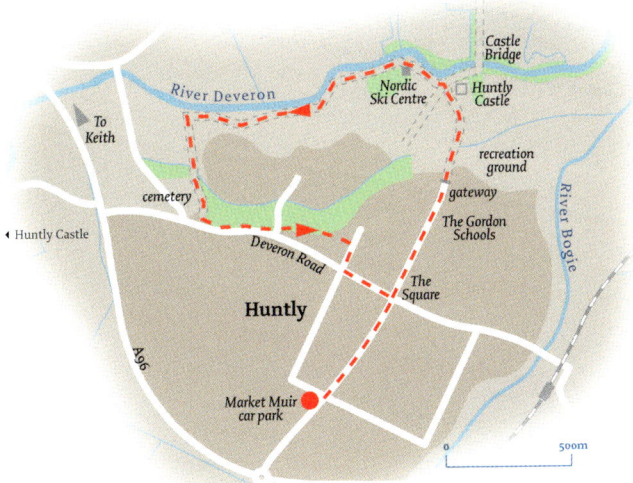

The original castle built on the site reportedly gave refuge to Robert the Bruce in the 14th century. After 1800, it fell into ruin and was heavily plundered for stone by local builders. It is now owned by Historic Scotland and is well worth a visit.

Follow the road round the left side of the castle and then double back to cross the stone bridge, following the sign for the Nordic & Outdoor Centre. Cross to the far end of the car park, go past the gate and take the path through the riverside park. When the surfaced path curves left, leave it to continue ahead on a path next to the River Deveron. The Outdoor Centre is passed on the left where artificial tracks allow people to practise Nordic or crosscountry skiing all year round.

The Deveron is one of the top five salmon fishing rivers in Scotland. It rises in the Ladder Hills before joining the River Bogie just below Huntly Castle, eventually flowing into the Moray Firth between the twin towns of Banff and Macduff.

Keep following the riverbank past a round sculpted seat and continue on the cycleway alongside the river. Stay on the cycleway as it curves left away from the river on a raised embankment. After a wooden fence turn left at a T-junction by the cemetery alongside the high stone wall with mature trees on the left. Keep straight ahead to rejoin the cycleway and follow it left as it runs alongside the road. Cross over Riverside Drive and continue past the next junctions before turning right down Meadow Street opposite a postbox. At Deveron Road, turn left to return to the square and retrace your steps to the start.

89

Clashmach Hill

Distance 7.25km **Time** 2 hours
Terrain grassy track, path, sometimes
muddy **Map** OS Explorer 425
Access regular trains and buses from
Aberdeen, Inverurie and Inverness
to Huntly

Huntly is a good place to while away an
afternoon or so. Surrounded by rich
farmland, it is famed for its shortbread
makers and boasts an annual food festival
as well as the popular Nordic & Outdoor
Centre. In the winter months, this high
section of North Aberdeenshire can be
severely hit by snow – crosscountry skis
could be a sensible option at times.

This walk starts from the Market Muir
car park on George V Avenue, on the left
side of the A97 on the way into Huntly.

From the centre of town, it can be reached
by following Gordon Street south from
the square. From the car park, follow the
A97 out of town, past the supermarket, to
the roundabout on the bypass. Turn right
here and carefully cross to the far side of
the busy A96, soon turning left up the
minor road signed for Tullochbeg. This
passes the auction mart which, as well as
doing a roaring trade in cattle, farm
machinery and the like, has a good café
open to everyone.

Follow the road uphill and, at the sharp
bend in just under 1km, continue straight
ahead, passing to the right of a bungalow
and onto a grassy path. Follow this
between bushes, passing a bench with
views back to Huntly, and continue past a
small mast towards a wind turbine.

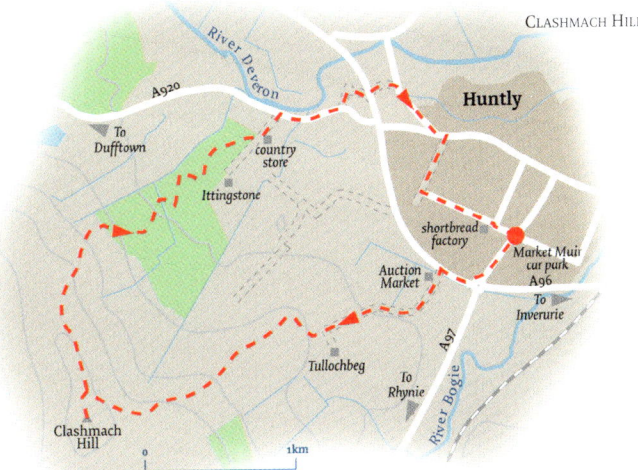

After a bend to the left, the path climbs more directly and the fields become rougher. Go through a gate and keep heading uphill to the left of the fence. A second gate leads to a path which takes you up to the ridge where there is an unexpected view of Ben Rinnes, the highest peak in the area, in front of the great mass of the Cairngorms. At a track, turn left, but make a mental note of this spot as you'll need to return the same way.

The summit is marked by a cairn and trig point and is a surprisingly good vantage point for the whole area, with Huntly spread out below, its castle visible near the River Deveron. The distinctive peaks of Tap o' Noth and Bennachie are also easy to pick out. Peregrines nest nearby so keep an eye out for one of these wheeling overhead.

Return through the last gate passed on the way up and immediately turn left. Follow the path which runs through the gorse, keeping the fence on your left. After 500m, the path veers away from the fence to head downhill. Go through a gate part way down and then another to follow a track that zigzags down through an area of young native trees. Ignore any paths to the right and left and continue over sometimes muddy ground to reach a gate. Go through this and turn left to reach the A920. Turn right for 400m of verge walking to a tarmac lane on the left; take this and turn right soon after to pass under the A96. At a T-junction, turn right to shortly reach Deveron Road (A920); cross this, turn left and pick up the cycleway running behind the houses to the right. Follow this until the end of the housing and head left, passing Dean's shortbread factory before bearing right after the fire station to return to the Market Muir car park.

Tap o' Noth

Distance 5km **Time** 2 hours **Terrain** grassy
tracks; steady climb to exposed moorland
summit **Map** OS Explorer OL62
Access no public transport to the start

The conspicuous summit of Tap o' Noth
is crowned by the second highest hillfort
in Scotland. The fairly strenuous ascent is
rewarded with stunning views and the
chance to poke about the impressive ruins
that could be up to 2000 years old.

Tap o' Noth is 2km northwest of Rhynie
on the A941 to Dufftown – a road whose
main claim to fame is its regular
appearances in the winter traffic news
when it is blocked by snow. The car park
is found along a signed lane off the north
side of the road.

Begin the walk along the marked
footpath, passing through a kissing gate.
Further on the path leads through another
gate. Follow the path through the bushes

to the left, keeping parallel to the fence.
The route continues in this direction for
650m, becoming clearer underfoot. There
are good views across the countryside
towards the tor on the summit of The
Buck. As the route reaches yet another
gate, turn right uphill towards the dome-
like Tap o' Noth, keeping to the right of
the plantations and through a final gate.

The origins of the unusual name, Tap
o' Noth, are a little uncertain. Tap is Scots,
meaning 'top', and Noth probably refers
to the local farming area. According to
local folklore, a giant, Jock o' Noth, stole
the girlfriend of Jock o' Bennachie,
thereby starting a feud which ended in a
boulder being flung at Jock o' Noth – this
boulder, indented by a quick deflection
from the latter giant's foot, is still marked
on large-scale maps today.

Follow the grassy track as it climbs,
first to the left, before swinging right and

◄ The track up Tap o' Noth

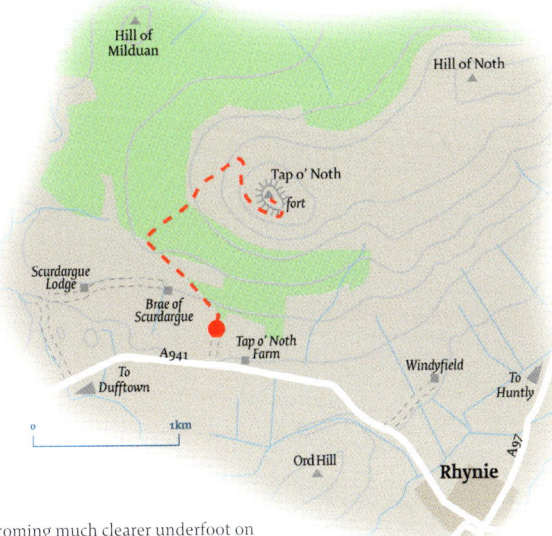

becoming much clearer underfoot on the final climb across the southern flank. From this approach, the wide-ranging views over rural Aberdeenshire are idyllic, a colourful patchwork of fields dotted with settlements, backed by the hills of Bennachie and Morven.

A gap in the eastern end of the fort is your portal into the Iron Age world – and the summit. Thought to be up to 2000 years old, the base walls are a strong band of vitrified stone. Huge fires must have been constructed to produce the immense heat needed to melt and fuse the stones; to this day, the actual method used remains an archaeological mystery. While the fort would have primarily been a defensive structure, the remains of what may have been wooden circular houses have been discovered, prompting speculation that people might have stayed on this inhospitable summit for substantial periods of time. The depression at the centre of the fort is thought to have been a water cistern.

The trig point marking the summit is found on the western edge of the wall. From here, Ben Rinnes is clearly visible with the Moray Firth beyond and The Buck nearer to hand. The return route is via the same outward path.

The Buck of Cabrach

Distance 4.6km **Time** 2 hours
Terrain boggy moorland, pathless in places, steady but fairly gentle climb
Map OS Explorer OL62
Access no public transport to the start

This conical hill ticks all the boxes for an enjoyable short hill walk – great views, straightforward navigation and a wild landscape. This route is rougher and higher than most others in this volume, so hillwalking gear, map and navigation skills are needed, as well as good boots as the route is very boggy in parts.

There is no official parking area for this walk; however, there is a suitable lay-by at the side of the B9002 between Lumsden and Cabrach, 800m south of the junction with the A941 at Elrick. Take care not to block any entrances or passing places.

From here, the pointy tor of The Buck beckons. Head south along the road briefly, from the parking area to a gate on the south side. Climb this and follow a faint track over deep heather.

At a fork keep left, soon bearing left on a narrow sheep trod to approach the remains of a fence which aims directly for the summit of The Buck. At the fence, the best path is on the far side; however, the going is extremely boggy whichever side you choose. As you gain height, the ground does improve underfoot, although there are still some very deep peat pools hidden in the heather – look out for the tell-tale sign of bright green moss. Looking back you can see the distinctive shapes of Tap o' Noth and Ben Rinnes.

Continue all the way to the summit, where the trig point stands atop a rocky

tor. There are extensive views over the patchwork grouse moors of Strathdon and the foothills of the Cairngorms and to the Moray Firth coast in the opposite direction. The summit also offers the chance to seek out a carved stone and an old boundary stone.

Look for a slab facing the trig point on the way to the top. Here, the sharp-eyed will find three interlocking carved fish, each with one eye and with initials above. Their origin is unknown, but archaeologists believe they are neither Pictish nor medieval – they may date from the 18th century and relate to a fishing society. You may find a visitors' book hidden in one of the walls near the summit; if you use it to record your ascent, remember to return it to its

hiding place as in the past walkers have mistaken it for someone's lunchbox. A large stone marks the boundary between the parishes of Auchindoir, Kearn and Kildrummy.

The return is a reversal of the outward climb – the bogs give you something to look forward to once you reach the lower ground en route to the road.

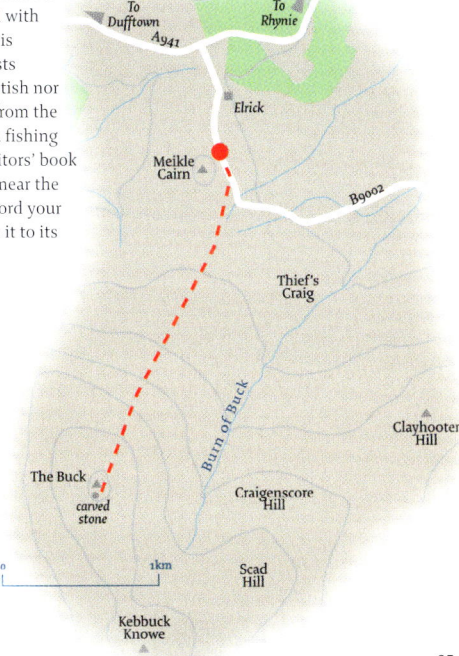

◀ The Buck, seen from Tap o' Noth

Index